Watching Nature

Watching the Moon

By Edana Eckart

Welcome Books™

Children's Press®
A Division of Scholastic Inc.
New York / Toronto / London / Auckland / Sydney
Mexico City / New Delhi / Hong Kong
Danbury, Connecticut

Photo Credits: Cover © Charles C. Place/Getty Images; p. 5 © Al III Petteway/Getty Images;
p. 7 © Digital Vision; pp. 9, 17 © SuperStock, Inc.; p. 11 © Rob Atkins/Getty Images; moon's
orbit illustrated by Michelle Innes; p. 13 © Siegfried Layda/Getty Images; p. 15 © Ken Ross/Getty
Images; p. 19 © Paul Edmondson/Getty Images

Contributing Editors: Shira Laskin and Jennifer Silate
Book Design: Michelle Innes

Library of Congress Cataloging-in-Publication Data

Eckart, Edana.
   Watching the moon / by Edana Eckart.
   p. cm.—(Watching nature)
   Summary: Simple text introduces facts about the moon.
   Includes bibliographical references and index.
   ISBN 0-516-27598-4 (lib. bdg.) ISBN 0-516-25936-9 (pbk.)
   1. Moon—Juvenile literature. [1. Moon.] I. Title.

QB582.E25 2004
523.3—dc21

                                    2003009113

Contents

The Moon is in the sky.

You can see it at night.

The Moon has holes in it called **craters**.

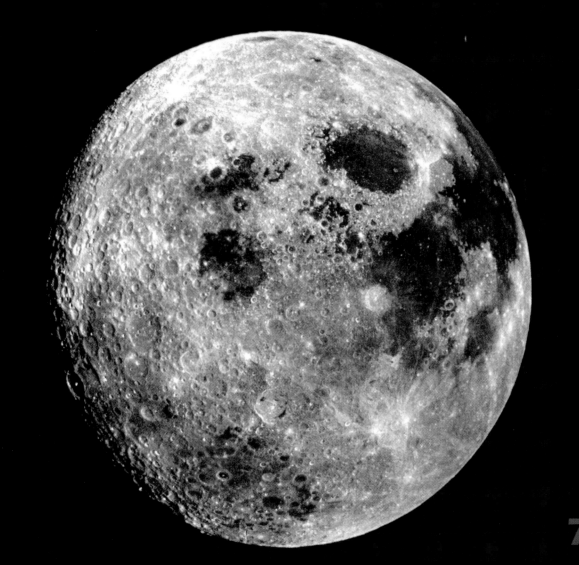

7

The Moon is a big circle tonight.

This is called a **full Moon**.

The Moon moves around Earth.

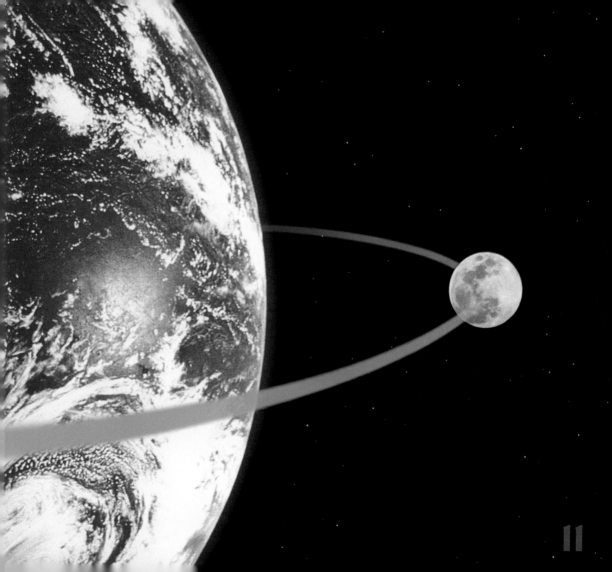

The Moon looks different at different times.

The Moon looks bigger when it is closer to Earth.

Sometimes, the Moon can look very small.

This is called a **crescent Moon**.

15

Sometimes you can only see **half** of the Moon.

This is called a half Moon.

17

Some nights, the Moon looks like it is not there at all.

This is called a **new Moon**.

19

The Moon makes the night sky beautiful.

21

New Words

craters (**kray**-turz) large holes in the ground
caused by something such as a bomb or other
falling objects

crescent Moon (**kress**-uhnt **moon**) the phase
of the Moon when it is a small, curved shape

full Moon (**ful moon**) the phase of the Moon when
the side turned toward Earth is entirely lit

half (**haf**) one of two equal parts of something

new Moon (**noo moon**) the phase of the Moon
when the side turned toward Earth is
entirely dark

To Find Out More

Books
So That's How the Moon Changes Shape!
by Allan Fowler
Scholastic Library Publishing

The Moon Book
by Gail Gibbons
Holiday House

Web Site
Nova: To the Moon
http://www.pbs.org/wgbh/nova/tothemoon/
Read many interesting things about the Moon and
people who have gone there on this Web site.

Index

About the Author
Edana Eckart has written several children's books. She enjoys bike riding with her family.

Reading Consultants
Kris Flynn, Coordinator, Small School District Literacy, The San Diego County Office of Education

Shelly Forys, Certified Reading Recovery Specialist, W.J. Zahnow Elementary School, Waterloo, IL

Paulette Mansell, Certified Reading Recovery Specialist, and Early Literacy Consultant, TX

'Paul Vidich's tense, muscular thriller delivers suspense and intelligence circa 1953: Korea, Stalin, the Cold War rage brilliantly, and the hall of mirrors confronting reluctant agent George Mueller reflects myriad questions: Just how personal is the political? Is the past ever past? *An Honorable Man* asks universal questions whose shadows linger even now. Paul Vidich's immensely assured debut, a requiem to a time, is intensely alive, dark, silken with facts, replete with promise'
– Jayne Anne Phillips, *New York Times* bestselling author of *Quiet Dell* and *Machine Dreams*

'*An Honorable Man* is that rare beast: a good, old-fashioned spy novel. But like the best of its kind, it understands that the genre is about something more: betrayal, paranoia, unease, and sacrifice. For a book about the Cold War, it left me with a warm, satisfied glow'
– John Connolly, #1 internationally bestselling author of *A Song of Shadows*

'A cool, knowing, and quietly devastating thriller that vaults Paul Vidich into the ranks of such thinking-man's spy novelists as Joseph Kanon and Alan Furst. Like them, Vidich conjures not only a riveting mystery but a poignant cast of characters, a vibrant evocation of time and place, and a rich excavation of human paradox'
– Stephen Schiff, writer and co-executive producer of *The Americans*

THE GOOD ASSASSIN

PAUL VIDICH

NO EXIT PRESS

First published in 2017 by No Exit Press,
an imprint of Oldcastle Books Ltd,
PO Box 394, Harpenden,
Herts, AL5 1XJ, UK
noexit.co.uk
@noexitpress

A CIP catalogue record for this book is available from the British Library.

ISBN
978-0-85730-110-9 (paperback)
978-0-85730-112-3 (ePub)

2 4 6 8 10 9 7 5 3 1

Typeset by Avocet Typeset, Somerton, Somerset TA11 6RT
in Minion Pro

Pr

For Joe and Arturo, with love

'Blessed are the dead
that the rain falls on'

– F. Scott Fitzgerald
The Great Gatsby

PART I

1

WASHINGTON DC, 1958

IT WAS ALL SET in motion over lunch at Harvey's when the director made a casual request that caught George Mueller off guard. The request came out of nowhere in the midst of the director's rambling on about the unfortunate state of affairs in Cuba. Mueller thought it an odd, but harmless favor, and it didn't require anything of him that he wasn't willing to freely give – but still it was unexpected.

'Toby Graham is a good man and good men are hard to keep. They get tired, or fed up with the goddamned bureaucracy we've become, or squeamish about the work, or they want a bigger house. They move on. We think he is leaving us. I want to know what's on his mind.'

It was noon. Mueller remembered the time well. The restaurant was empty at that hour and the director, who arrived early to the office, had taken to lunching before the place filled with a boisterous crowd of eavesdropping Capitol Hill staffers.

The director had drained his second gin martini right after the first.

Mueller had come down by train from New Haven for their annual lunch, which had started the year he left the Agency, and now five years on had devolved into a quaint ritual. Mueller didn't allow himself to look interested when the request came. He didn't want to give the director the satisfaction of seeing truth in his prediction that Mueller would become bored teaching privileged undergraduates, so he let the director make his case at length. Mueller listened indifferently and his expression had the flat affect of a judge at trial. The director held the last olive in his snaggletooth and withdrew the flagged toothpick, which he stuck in the warm French bread neither of them had touched. He slid an oyster into his mouth. He wore a slate blue suit with crimson pocket square and matching bow tie. He was older, but his effort to dress fashionably was young, and smart rimless spectacles rested on his thick nose. His gray hair had thinned and whatever he'd lost on his head now erupted from his eyebrows. The director shifted the conversation, as he was wont to do, to the unrelated topic of college teaching, going on at length on his theory of pedagogy.

'And that too,' the director said suddenly, 'is why I asked you here. You know how a man can change. Even the best of us miss the signs, and then when we see them we don't know whether to promote the change or contain it.'

Mueller didn't find the director's remark surprising. It was just like him to be vague and Mueller didn't take the trouble to respond.

'It's a small assignment,' the director said. 'A small favor. Probably a week of your time. You'll get paid well. I can be generous with people on the outside, and I'm sure you can use the extra income. Nothing dangerous or scandalous,' he assured Mueller.

'What's on Graham's mind?' the director repeated laconically. The emphasis implied by the repetition belied the casual tone of his voice. 'That's what I want to know. What's he thinking?'

'Thinking?'

'Is he happy? You know him, don't you?'

Mueller did know Graham. They'd been undergraduates together, where they met racing sculls, matched against each other on the Thames and the Connecticut River, beginning as rivals and remaining that way through the war, and then as colleagues in Vienna in '48. The director had their file and would know their history.

'I need someone I can trust,' the director said. 'Someone he will trust. Not an insider. Friends?'

'Friendly enough to grab a drink after work.'

'You still on the wagon?'

Mueller hated that phrase. What wagon? And why was being on the wagon synonymous with being sober? He was inclined to challenge the director on his choice of speech, but he knew wisdom in the English language lay in the simile, so he casually repeated, 'Still on the wagon.' He lifted his half-finished Coca Cola to prove his claim. 'Wine occasionally.'

'Campus life has been good for you. I don't trust men who won't drink with me.'

Mueller had heard the director use the line before. It was one of those repetitions that came unconsciously, and if you knew the person long enough you knew it was a tic that came out like a prejudice, but now the director's words lacked his usual cheerful mocking tone. He seemed preoccupied.

'We need to know what's on his mind,' the director said again. 'You're familiar with his type of work.'

Mueller didn't need an explanation, for these things were known among the men who shared the fraternity of intelligence. To ask a question was to suggest a suspicion. Trust was the fragile bond that held them together. Agents did things that made them useful in the field, but memories were dangerous with men who left, retired, or were forced out. Details of covert operations. Compromising reports of unfortunate mistakes. The truth beneath plausible denials. Agents stuck together, but that was not who Mueller was. He had stayed away from his old colleagues except for his annual lunch with the director.

'We can't erase a man's memory, but we can judge his loyalty.' The director looked at Mueller and an evanescent smile broke through his grim visage. 'He may want to take time off. Like you. He's been working hard.'

The director lowered his voice as two Capitol Hill staffers walked by, and he leaned toward Mueller, close enough for Mueller to smell the cloying alcohol. His cheeks had a rosy, happy blush. Mueller thought the director had aged in the intervening year – gained weight, eyes dimmed, lost his smugness – worn down by the bitter rivalries among temperamental politicians who called him to confess before closed-door congressional hearings.

'You will work with the FBI's man in Havana. Frank Pryce.'

The director pushed a file toward Mueller, and Mueller didn't push it back, which was a mistake. When he saw the yellow-stamped 'top secret' and 'eyes only' he found himself uncomfortably reluctant to give them up. An old adrenaline conspired against his hesitation.

'We've gotten over the rivalries,' the director said. 'That soap opera doesn't play well with the White House. We won the turf war so now we can be magnanimous. They can be useful here. If there is a success they can take credit and we won't have to dirty our hands.'

The file before Mueller described Pryce's discovery – suspicion, the director amended when he saw Mueller raise an eyebrow.

'Pryce believes the arms embargo against Batista has been breached. Weapons are getting through. There has been a lot of self-righteous chest-beating on Capitol Hill that we put guns in the hands of a dictator who turned them on his citizens. Congress and the press whine that our State Department's noble intentions with the embargo came too late, offered too little. That we're coddling a tyrant.' The director smiled. 'Our public outrage against dictators we secretly prop up is one of our glorious hypocrisies.' He licked the last drop of gin from his glass. 'Pryce thinks it's Graham.'

The director looked at Mueller. 'Pryce won't give his sources. The mob? Hotel wiretaps?' The director arched an eyebrow. 'I want to know what Pryce knows. I want to know what he thinks is going on.' He nodded. 'You try and find out.'

He popped the last olive in his mouth. 'We can't be ostriches about this. Has Graham become a risk? Has he gone around the embargo on his own? We hire good men and give them latitude. It goes without saying that Graham shouldn't know we are asking questions.'

Mueller tolerated the director's continued presumption that he'd take the assignment, and he knew that each time he didn't object he compromised his ability to decline.

'Pryce will have the details. He knows what we want. Batista's people are in the dark.'

Disdain and scorn rose in the director's voice when he mentioned the Cuban dictator by name. 'Abjectly corrupt. A fat worthless head of state. God knows how we pick our allies.'

Mueller didn't agree to the assignment at their lunch, but his silence was confederate to the director's request. He knew one week was an impossibly optimistic estimate of the time he'd be in Cuba, but the idea that he would escape campus lethargy had tart appeal. His sabbatical was upon him, but he'd lost interest in his research on the puns and paradoxes in *Hamlet*, a lively but binocularly narrow topic, and he was out of sorts with his life. He had arrived at New Haven and was disappointed by the petty academic squabbling, and in his first year he had found that he had time on his hands, was prone to being morose, and longed for the clarity of his old job. He poured his deep ambivalence about the conduct of the Cold War spy game, and how it sacrificed good men for abstract principles, into two paperback novels that were transparently autobiographical, thinking it was a way to make a little money. Teaching and his writing had been a retirement that appealed to his solitary personality, but in time he saw himself as his ex-colleagues saw him, a middle-aged man who belonged to that tragic class of spy prematurely removed from the game – for whom academic life thickened the waist and atrophied instincts. A chess master suddenly withdrawn from a championship match to a rural Connecticut life.

Mueller had stood back from campus life, as he had learned to do in the field, but being an outsider – essential for a spy – made it hard to be a civilian. He'd been appalled to discover that he'd exchanged the rank hypocrisy of Agency work for petulant campus politics.

'I'm happy where I am,' he said to the director. They stood on the sidewalk outside Harvey's. 'I don't have the time for this.'

'If he is your friend,' he said, 'you should do this. Lockwood made your arrangements.'

They parted quietly. The sun was high. Its lurid glare scorched the street. They walked in opposite directions into the sparse population out in Washington's oppressive humidity. Mueller was lanky and handsome, but nondescript in a gray suit, and boyish even in his robust middle age. He felt no urgency in life and no zeal, at least not any longer, and all this gave him a blandness that didn't draw the stranger's eye as he strolled to Union Station.

*

Mueller met CIA Inspector General Lockwood a week later in the Rockefeller Center offices of *Holiday* magazine. Lockwood knew the editor, an old OSS colleague who'd agreed to hire Mueller to write an article on Havana's night life so he'd have a cover story.

It was a lunch meeting in a private dining room on the thirty-eighth floor that looked north to Central Park. Throughout the one hour Mueller's eyes drifted to the panoramic view of that great rectangle of landscape design wedged between Fifth Avenue's Beaux Arts mansions and Central Park West's gothic co-ops. *A shoebox of greenery,* he thought. Mueller looked for the metaphor in things. The right image, he told his students, was an aid to unreliable memory.

'George?' Lockwood said. 'You're distracted. We need your full attention if you're going to be a success here.'

Mueller took his eyes off the canopy of trees. 'Thinking about Graham.'

Mueller had met Lockwood when he was division chief

positioned for a senior leadership role in the Agency, and then he contracted polio during a trip to Asia on Agency business that left him paralyzed from the waist down. He was a protégé of the director, who accommodated his handicap and made him inspector general, a fittingly senior staff job and suitable for a man confined to a wheelchair, but a dead end. Mueller had been impressed by Lockwood's stoic dignity. Not once had he seen the man angry, resentful, or depressed. He was the same lanky WASP with his spit of unruly blond hair he brushed from his forehead, but all of him was now compressed into a black mechanical chassis he wheeled around with gloved hands.

'You were talking about the FBI,' Mueller said, looking at Lockwood, who was opposite him at the dining table laid with serviettes, silverware, bone china, and a flower centerpiece. Mueller met Lockwood's skeptical gaze with a benign smile. Though he disapproved of the FBI's aggressive tactics, and their altogether too heartfelt policing, he had it in him, he said, to cooperate. Dignity, formality, self-restraint. Gifts he allowed himself to believe he had. 'I can work with them. We're all mature here.'

Mueller knew that Lockwood performed liaison work with the FBI through the president's Foreign Intelligence Agency Board, and he was the architect of a rapprochement between the CIA and the FBI. How had he put it on their way up the elevator? 'Intelligence has to be divorced from police work otherwise a Gestapo is created. We are separate but we cooperate. We've got the president yelling he wants someone to tell him what the hell is going on in Cuba. There are people from all over the place, different agencies, different interests, including the FBI, telling him different things, so this is all about that.'

This? Mueller had asked.

'The FBI is in Havana bugging hotel rooms where the mob stays – Lansky and Stassi and Trafficante. Taped conversations that the FBI makes into transcripts. They don't know that we know, and they don't know that we've discovered through our own channels that they think we may be responsible for those weapons. You can't imagine the shit storm in the White House if the director of the FBI walked into the Oval Office with secret recordings that showed one of our assets was ignoring the State Department embargo. We are staying close to the FBI. Friends close, enemies closer, right, George?'

'A bunch of spleeny dog-hearted farts.' This from the editor.

Mueller turned to the man seated prominently at the head of the table. He almost laughed. As the one not drinking, Mueller was aware of the volume consumed by the other two. Mueller wondered how the editor would do anything productive when he got back to his desk. He had heard the man's voice deepen with alcohol and then his humor had thickened too. He was a corpulent man, with thinning hair and piercing blue eyes. Lockwood had given Mueller background on the editor during the elevator ride. He was part of the original OSS contingent who'd come over to the Agency and chafed at the new rules. He became fed up with the growing bureaucracy and was deeply ambivalent about the conduct of the Cold War, and he'd left after the Korean Armistice, taking with him his resentments, his drinking, his opinions, which he offered freely as an editor – and he had his targets. He despised the head of the FBI and denounced him as an incontinent paranoid. England was another target for his readers: 'Crumbling cold water castles not fit to sleep in.'

The editor looked at Mueller. 'I read your book. The writing is tolerable. Good enough for us. I'm looking for color on that worm of an island that sits below the Florida Keys.' The editor said he needed a new angle. 'Everyone says it's dangerous, but our readers want to visit and they need to believe it's safe. They want a week in the Caribbean away from humdrum lives – to gamble, to drink, and to watch erotic floor shows – the taste of scandal they don't get at home.'

The editor winked at Mueller. He added sternly, 'I don't want a police report with body counts. Advertisers won't pay for that. Don't invent anything, of course, but you don't have to harp on the bombings. Isn't that guy Castro stuck in the mountains?'

The editor rang the waiter's bell. Lunch was over. He finished the conversation with a suggestion. 'Hemingway is there in Finca Vigía. Find out what he thinks of Castro. He's a man dedicated to his art and has an equivalent dedication to everything he does, his fishing, his drinking, and he's a serious guy who is horrified by the shoddy, the fraudulent, the sentimental, the haphazard, the immoral. So, he is a man of strong opinions and he must have an opinion on Castro. Put the question to him. I'll double your word rate if you get a quote out of him.'

*

Within the week George Mueller found himself aboard PAN AM Flight 29 with two reporter's notebooks, a letter of introduction, and the ambiguous comfort of a return trip ticket traveling to that season's war zone. Toby Graham was in Mueller's mind when Idlewild Airport sank beneath the airplane, and he was still in his thoughts hours later when the stewardess nodded at his empty glass. 'Last call.' She pointed out the window. 'The Sierra Maestra.' She took a moment to chat and guessed he was a lawyer, which he was not. She pegged his age at forty, which was close, and she thought he was married, which was half right. Divorced years before. 'The Tropic of Cancer is there,' she said. 'We are a tropical country, but there it is alpine.' She pointed to the east at the deep green toupee of hunched peaks penetrating the low cloud cover.

Mueller looked down. A vast savanna opened up below the plane and the overriding impression was of a linear order imposed on the land by dirt roads and barbed-wire fences formed into rectangles of pastureland. Geometry imposed on the land was broken where ancient flows gave meandering course to streams that fed a larger river. And then a change in air pressure and he knew their descent to Havana had begun.

The stewardess took his empty glass. Yes, she had come on to him, but when he showed little interest, she walked away and his thoughts returned to Toby Graham. For all his hours of contemplation during the flight, Mueller had no better insight in the stubborn question the director had raised. Graham was a man shaped by espionage. He'd made an early reputation turning ex-Nazis and sending them back into East Germany. Some of them survived long enough to provide intelligence on Soviet military installations, but most were promptly caught and executed. Graham took to the practice of spying. He drew diagrams, planned covert operations, seemed to live in a continuous state of emergency, planted in their cold office in West Berlin most days for ten or twelve hours, or running off to Tempelhof Airport. He jogged in the morning. Drank in bars until late. Mueller saw these surface details in his mind's eye like a photograph that didn't open up – revealing little of the inner man.

2

DAIQUIRIS AND BOMBS

DRENCHING RAIN PULLED A veil over the face of the city. Mueller stood just inside the bar's door, as did a jolly, middle-aged American couple, who had also been caught in the sudden downpour and laughed brightly at the indignity of their misfortune. One week in Havana had bronzed Mueller's face and worn thin the novelty of the place.

He slapped his sturdy straw hat against his thigh, knocking off water, and his darting eyes made a confirming survey of the customers. Ever since he'd left the Agency Mueller had tried to unwind his habit of surveying a bar before he sat down, but now he was glad he had the old habit. His eyes drifted from one table to the next, as he raked his hair, taking in each face to see if he knew the person, or to discover if a customer took an interest in him, and if one did, because of some chance encounter, Mueller was prepared to account for his presence, and he had an explanation ready.

It was too early for cocktails, except for the sullen man alone at the bar, whose drinking had no clock, and several sailors on shore leave from the U.S. Navy frigate anchored in the harbor. Across the room half a dozen Cubans were gathered around a table, and they had taken notice when Mueller arrived, but they'd gone back to their conspiratorial whispers. A radio played 'Volare.'

Mueller glanced at his watch. Toby Graham was late. Graham had been abrupt on the phone – after he got over his surprise – and he asked if they could talk in person at El Floridita. One of those shoddy Havana saloons where the food is cheap and the drinks generous. The word 'shoddy' had stuck in Mueller's mind, and it repeated itself as he took in the place. Red velvet cushions on the banquettes were worn thin, or missing, and the ceiling fan made a labored squeak with each slow revolution. Framed celebrity photographs hung askew on a wall of flies.

Mueller's eyes wandered across the gallery of Hollywood actors. He liked to think of himself as someone who could both quote Hamlet and put a name to that year's popular movie stars. His little private conceit. There was Errol Flynn from *The Sea Hawk*, a movie he knew only by reputation, and there was Ava Gardner, her bare shoulders and alluring smile from *The Killers*, which he had seen, but had not liked. And he picked out John Wayne, George Raft, Stewart Granger, Orson Welles, Deborah Kerr, Richard Burton, and he felt good about his score, but then he stopped at the last photograph. There was a burly man, bordering on heavy, on a dock, whose face was obscured by the shadow of a wide straw hat.

'Hemingway,' a voice said. 'He's standing next to a big dead fish.'

Mueller turned. He recognized all at once the buzz-cut, the wrinkled white linen suit, the big man thick in the waist like a

23

tree trunk who stood before him as if he'd taken root.

'You look surprised. Some people aren't good with names.'

'Frank Pryce,' Mueller said civilly.

Pryce laughed. 'I meant Hemingway. I suppose you could have forgotten my name.'

Mueller didn't let Pryce see that his surprise had nothing to do with names.

'Grab a drink,' Pryce said. 'Wait out the storm. Or a sandwich, if you haven't eaten.'

Mueller struggled with the algebra of rudeness, but the FBI man coaxed him forward and Mueller found himself face-to-face across a table with the one man with whom he didn't want to be seen. He glanced at his watch again. *Think.*

'Papa Doble,' Pryce said to the waiter who'd appeared as soon as they were seated. 'Papa Doble. Understand? *Comprende?*'

Mueller waved off an order when the waiter looked at him.

'I'm not interrupting anything, am I?' Pryce asked.

Mueller shook his head rather than invent a lie. Pryce had the square jaw of a high school linebacker who'd gained weight in a desk job. A small gut folded over his tightly cinched belt and his linen suit had darkened from moisture. Beads of sweat dotted his hairline and his teeth clenched a cigarette that looked small on his puffy face. Mueller had formed a view of Pryce in their one meeting, and this second encounter reinforced the first impression that Pryce was of that loud class of overseas Americans who felt entitled to order a drink in English and to be irritated when the waiter didn't understand. There was that other thing too from the meeting held in Pryce's cubicle in the embassy where he'd summoned Mueller and then made him wait half an hour. That had put Mueller in a foul mood, and none of the smiling, pretend friendliness Pryce later exhibited got

Mueller to recover his goodwill. He listened to Pryce's summary of the state of play in Cuba. Castro's forces had turned back Batista's summer offensive in the Sierra Maestra mountains so now the chaotic opposition forces had no choice but to follow the lead of Castro's July 26th Movement. The name, he said, when Mueller asked, commemorated the date Castro attacked Moncada Barracks in 1953. Not much was accomplished after his brisk report. A goal agreed, the rules of the game set – when and how to communicate, each keeping the other informed of what he did. Easy promises of cooperation.

Pryce nodded at the tall, cold drink that landed on the table. 'Papa Doble. House specialty. Hemingway sits over there in the corner and orders three at a time. One puts the ordinary drinker in a blissful state, but he does three. Immense daiquiris with grapefruit juice instead of lime. Sailors approach him having read his books on a long ocean voyage hoping to shake the hand of the man who won the Nobel Prize.'

Mueller shook his head when he was offered a taste.

'I read your novel,' Pryce said. 'What's it called? *Judas Hour*? Not even the tradecraft was believable. Poison toothpaste? It made me wonder if you'd ever worked in the field.'

Mueller felt his cheeks flush. The incident Pryce brought up only to disparage was from the beginning of the novel when the main character is dispatched on a mission to assassinate a popularly elected African president. Mueller had struggled to fill the lacunae when a stubborn Agency censor deleted a classified killing technique.

'The false detail spoiled the rest of the book.' Pryce affected preoccupation with his cigarette, holding it before him, studying it, then again put it between clenched teeth. Mueller watched him finish the entire cigarette without removing it, ash lengthening, drooping, falling in clumps on his cotton shirt as he spoke. Sometimes he brushed away the ashes, but he continued to offer his literary critique with the cigarette dangling from his lips. When he accused Mueller of being inauthentic he snatched the cigarette with his fingers so he could apply the full force of his speech.

'I expected something better from you.' Pryce set his drink down carefully on the coaster, centering it, then slowly raised his eyes. 'I followed you here, you know.'

Mueller raised his eyes. 'Oh.'

'I was across the street. I saw someone leave the portico and run with a newspaper over his head. Then I saw it was you. I lowered my car window and yelled, but you didn't hear me. I wondered what was so urgent that you'd leave a dry spot. I thought, hell, he's got his interview with Hemingway.'

Mueller remembered what Lockwood had said. *He's a homesick man trying to keep busy.* He felt the conversation lengthening. 'Nothing better to do? No crooks to shake down?'

'No shortage of things for me to do, George. Plenty to keep me busy. The mob. You guys keep me busy.' He paused. 'Toby Graham keeps me busy. He's stationed mid-island but I hear he's in Havana now. Have you caught up with him?'

Mueller was silent.

'Remarkable man. Dangerous man. Hard to pin down what he does, but by what people say of him, all the things, he could be two men. One person couldn't do all of it. Men like him are put in the field and expected to use their judgment. It's their willingness to push the edge of things that makes them good. Has he crossed the line? There's talk he's a hit man.'

The words made the nerves on the back of Mueller's neck constrict. They were rarely seen in Agency memoranda, and if used at all, it was done allusively. No one wanted to acknowledge or admit to state murder. The director had not suggested it. Lockwood raised doubt without passing judgment by using the anodyne: *Our options are limited.*

'Sounds like you know what you need to know.' Mueller felt himself being tested. Mueller looked directly at Pryce. 'I'm not sure what I'm doing here. Maybe I should take the next flight home.'

Pryce exhaled from the corner of his mouth. He affected pleasantness. 'You guys in the CIA are a smug Ivy League bunch.'

'I'm not one of them,' Mueller said coldly. 'I don't have a stake in this. You want my help? Happy to help. Happy to let you figure it out by yourself too. But don't mistake why I'm here. Or who I am.'

Mueller looked at his watch again and made no effort to hide his impatience. 'I think we're done here.'

Pryce stared. He looked around the bar and his eyes settled back on Mueller. 'You're meeting him. Is that what's going on?'

'He asked to see me. Alone.'

Pryce stood. He hitched his belt over his lumpish gut and thrust his shoulders back like a displaying turkey. He looked at Mueller, then glanced around the bar again. 'You don't know half the trouble he is in.'

On the radio, a Mexican song with bright brassy instrumentation and whoops and whistles had just ended. There came a sad song of plucked and strummed instruments accompanied by tenors singing melancholy lyrics with the refrain, *Mama son de la loma.* The bartender reached over to the radio and raised the volume.

Suddenly a Cuban among the seated group leapt to his feet. He was a slight man in a baggy suit, young, gentlemanly, a bit reserved, with a trimmed moustache and beaked nose. He had sprung from his seat like a jack-in-the-box. His wiry frame was board stiff, his voice strident, and he yelled toward the sailors, *'Abajo el tirano. Abajo el dictador.'*

'Now there will be trouble,' Pryce said laconically. He dropped his cigarette to the floor and ground it with his heel.

Startled customers became alert. The American couple looked up from their Havana guide book. Other Cubans at the table rose from their chairs, and added a loud chorus of *Abajo el dictador.*

A burly waiter hustled the Cuban provocateur out of the bar. Waiters moved among the tables solicitous, chagrined, apologizing. 'He was referring to Franco, of course.'

Suddenly, a detonation rattled the quiet of the afternoon. A brilliant fiery flash went off outside the bar. It was followed instantly by a massive concussive blast that blew out the bar's plate glass window and left the floor littered with broken red and white wine bottles so the floor was the color of rose. A hint of alcohol in the air mixed with the sweet sulfur odor of explosives.

A profound quiet settled around Mueller. Anguished faces of the injured in the room were mute. And then the knobs inside his head that control hearing turned up and everywhere he heard desperate pleas for help.

Pryce touched his shoulder. 'You okay?'

Mueller realized he was sitting on the floor and he had no memory of how he'd gotten there. He cupped his ears and gently rocked his head to silence the ringing. He was surprised not to find blood.

'Don't go out,' Pryce said. 'They time the second bomb to follow the first.'

Waiters had gathered at the smashed window and cautiously

looked beyond the jagged glass that formed the hole. The American held his wife's hand, which bled profusely where a projectile of flying glass had neatly sliced through the wrist so it now hung by a tendon.

Mueller rose and made for the door, to escape, or observe, he wasn't sure.

'Stay put,' Pryce shouted. 'No one should go out until the police have cleaned the street. You can't be of any help. The country has to burn a little before it gets its sense back.'

Mueller saw Pryce use his belt as a tourniquet on the woman's arm and settle the numbed husband with a few calming instructions. Mueller paused, surprised by Pryce's gesture, and seeing that side of the man made Pryce more human – more dangerous.

Mueller stepped outside. Already it was chaotic in the street. The grim tableau of violence was softened by the steaming vapor of the drenching rain rising off the hot asphalt. A milk truck had been reduced to its axle and the rest of the vehicle was gone, vaporized. Radiating from the mangled chassis were crates, broken bottles, and pooled milk thinned by the rain. Overturned cars formed a perimeter around the blast zone.

Mueller walked in the soaking rain among the injured. The face of terror was always the same. Injured bystanders sat stunned on the sidewalk, and he moved from one to the next with his offer of help. The dead were obvious. Body parts were scattered about, as if left by a tide – a naked leg severed at the hip still with its high heel shoe. A pregnant woman with a gash on her cheek. Her dress had lost a strap and one breast hung free. Mueller covered her shoulders with his sport jacket.

Pouring rain blurred the edges of violence and only approaching sirens brought Mueller back to the moment.

Police arrived first, and within minutes the ambulances, and then shortly afterward the green Oldsmobiles of the Servicio de Inteligencia Militar. SIM officers went about cordoning off the blast site with a perimeter to hold back the crowd gathering under the portico. They wielded cudgels against bystanders who ventured too close to the smoldering debris. From time to time one of these men in tan uniforms culled a bystander and dragged him to a paddy wagon. Pale blue uniforms of the regular police inspired respect from the crowd, but the tan uniforms of SIM inspired fear. One or two young boys knew what to expect and backed away. The crowd knew how to react to the threat. Everywhere cautious people hung back.

Mueller saw a young girl barely to puberty grabbed by a SIM officer. Her sly retreat toward a side alley indicted her. The thuggish officer struck once on her back with the sound of a crack. Her face curled in pain. She wore sandals, a loose dress, and long hair that he pulled. Mueller thought she was his son's age.

He saw the officer strike again. She was too small, too frail, too childlike to resist. The sight stirred him from his complacency. He turned away from the girl, but her screams continued. Mueller cursed the impulse that rose in him. He had trained to be indifferent, to be cautious, to inure himself to the terrible things in the world.

'Enough,' he said. He stood tall, dignified, a surprising authority over the stocky officer. 'She is a girl. Una joven.'

The officer, startled at the intervention, paused to take the measure of the man challenging him.

'She did nothing,' Mueller said, seeing he had the officer's attention.

The officer gave Mueller a blasphemous look that said he could do what he wanted to the girl. She had already hunched over against the coming blow. Mueller grabbed the officer's forearm and stopped his swing from landing.

He was promptly arrested. Tan-uniformed SIM surrounded Mueller and handcuffed him. He tried to be calm as he was dragged to the paddy wagon and placed among other handcuffed men. Mueller saw the girl lying on the sidewalk like a broken doll. He also saw Frank Pryce, who'd seen the whole episode from the bar. He stood in the doorway, arms akimbo. His face had a flat expression that revealed the burden of his contempt.

Gray light in the paddy wagon was extinguished when the double doors were slammed shut. Faces of men inside were illuminated only with the cab's peephole. The closeness of their bodies, dank with sweat and rain, made the men less human. Faces around Mueller were grim, eyes wide, fear palpable. The man across from Mueller had the toughened expression of a prisoner rallying courage against coming indignities. Mueller saw he was the same man who'd jumped from his seat like a jack-in-the-box.

Mueller knew there was nothing to do but allow himself to go through with the arrest. Press credentials in his pocket would provide some measure of protection.

Mueller recalled Pryce's comment that the country had to burn a little. It was the sort of thing Toby Graham would say, to justify the violence. Graham had always been one of those men whose dedication to work took him into the darkness, and as a matter of course, doing the work he did, he brought some measure of darkness into himself. How do you keep the darkness from consuming your humanity? Mueller had seen it, he'd feared it, avoided it, and he recognized it. There were rumors about Graham. Terrible things he'd organized, administered, deployed, carried out in Guatemala. Did he have a hand in this?

3

HOTEL NACIONAL

'SHE WAS A DOPEY blonde.'

Mueller sat on a sofa in the Hotel Nacional's vast marble lobby with an espresso that he sipped parsimoniously to play out the little drink for his conversation with the woman at his side, who flipped photographs of her portfolio and accompanied each with a remark. He leaned forward to get a better look at the bikini model at the wheel of the pink Cadillac convertible. He tried his best to be impressed.

The photographer wore cuffed pants, camouflage utility vest, and a 35mm silver Leica around her shoulder, like a handbag. She had a boyish body, a wisp of a woman whose sunglasses were entirely too large for her face, and a ponytail. 'She wouldn't cooperate. It's about the car, I told her, but she kept acting as if it was about her face.'

Mueller was subdued. He tried to see merit in the way the breeze had caught the model's hair to convey the charm of a luxury car, and in the next photo he pretended to like how a cigarette in a woman's poised fingers captured her sex. He listened to the photographer explain how her work in advertising made her competent to capture the spirit of Havana. Mueller wanted an honest picture of the city to accompany his article, he said, and he wanted to know how the glossy tear sheets were evidence of her eye for grit.

Suddenly, Mueller heard his name called. He looked across the crowded lobby, eyes sweeping the archipelago of rush chairs that dotted the room. His name again, brightly spoken, clear like struck crystal. There she was at the bank of French doors open to the gardens and a view of the Caribbean. She stood by a weeping palm just inside a half-circle of chest-high sandbags.

'George!'

Her hand was raised above her head, and she was motionless, like a statue. She wore snug jodhpurs that flared at the hip and a blindingly bright blouse that filled with sea breeze. Her face was tan and thinned by tropical heat and she looked right at Mueller. When she saw that she'd caught his eye her hand waved vibrantly.

'We were so worried.' She stopped short of him, face beaming, ambivalent about how close to get. She took him in, the whole of him, and her hand covered her mouth. A short gasp escaped her lips. 'What's that?'

'This?' Mueller's hand touched an angry bump above his eye crowned with a cut closed with several stitches. 'They couldn't resist getting in a good shot before they let me go.' He lifted his bruised hand. 'It's nothing. The embassy has a doctor on call who came to my hotel. He said if they wanted to hurt me I'd be in the morgue. I'll live. How are you?'

Her hand came off her face. 'That's terrible.'

'Terribly lucky.'

'You didn't mention it on the phone.'

'Doubtful what you see be true unless confirmed with ocular proof.'

'Oh, stop it, George. This is serious. You haven't changed a bit. Same smug humor. Hug me.'

Mueller took Liz Malone in his arms, sweeping her up in a brief friendly hug she was returning. The drama of the lobby, the excitement of the reunion, and her glowing smile stirred his memory of their old entanglements. They looked in each other's eyes, fixed and staring for a moment. She suddenly pulled away, uncomfortable. She stepped back and spoke politely. 'Jack pulled every string he could to free you. He called up Washington. He got the ambassador involved. He made a big stink.'

Mueller was suddenly aware they were not alone. His training prepared him to know everything about a room while pretending only to see the person he spoke to, and he felt a presence behind before the hand touched his shoulder.

'Chico, how are you?'

Mueller was face to face with a broadly smiling Jack Malone. The man's fingers worked a hard massage into Mueller's muscles in the unwanted way of an old friend acting out a college locker room greeting. Jack nicknamed everyone he met as a way of owning a relationship. Mueller had always hated being called Chico.

'You got yourself into a big fix, old boy. You're lucky I got you out before they wired your balls to a generator. Or put a bullet in your head. One dead American is all the pretext the embassy needs to call in the marines.'

Mueller smiled. The same old Jack, he thought. Likable and

34

unlikable in equal measure, but always predictable, and in the long years of an acquaintance there was something to be said for knowing he hadn't changed. They'd circled each other freshman year wary of their different backgrounds, which acted like repelling magnets, Mueller the product of public school and Jack the Texas boy sent to New England prep schools by a New York socialite mother who had been dragged to Houston by her oil man husband. Mueller had been drawn to Jack's big personality, so different from his own reserve. The ruddy color in Jack's face had been there in college and never left – perhaps because he spent so many summers in the hot Texas sun and now, years later, his features were set and he would be that way until he died. His red hair might fade without turning gray, and his skin tone lighten, but his face would look the same. He was a tall man, with a classic build, who'd been good at sports in school and kept his body fit with a rancher's active life. He knew he was attractive to women. Mueller had seen it in college and that idea of himself persisted after marriage. Mueller had seen it coming after Liz and Jack married young and a decade passed without children. He'd seen Jack's affinity for pretty young girls – and Jack had been open about it in private conversations over drinks, when they talked about their lives. He said he liked the company of young women. They amused him, he said, diverted him, stimulated him.

'You're safe now,' Jack said. 'For the moment at least. Don't think you can play God here. Different rules.' Jack embraced his old friend and took a step back to observe Mueller. 'So,' he said. 'What is it you said brought you down?'

'Writing an article.'

'Who for?'

'*Holiday.*'

'I've heard of them. Still trying to turn bored freshmen into brilliant thinkers? Or you give up that too?'

Mueller felt old grudges stir.

'Oh, come on, George, lighten up. Let's get a drink. Girls, let's have a drink. We need to get you out to the ranch. You'll see the other Cuba.'

Same old Jack, Mueller thought. Loud, pugnacious, confident, thinking he was more charming than he was. There was no social gathering not made better by alcohol. When the drinks came, he lifted his scotch whiskey. 'To your health, George. What's left of it.' He nodded at the wound. 'They don't like to be interfered with. Fortunately, the men who run things here are practical.'

Liz smiled. 'You mean they can be bribed.'

Jack shrugged off the insinuation. 'He's free, that's what matters. He's free and he's safe.' To Mueller: 'The ambassador is a dilettante, but he owed me a favor so he helped with the head of the secret police. They don't call themselves secret police. That doesn't sound good in a democracy. They're called SIM, pronounced SEEM. I played you up as an important correspondent whom they wouldn't want to piss off. I told them they didn't need the scandal of you, George, found in a morgue hitting the front pages of America's finest newspapers. *Reporter murdered by Batista's police.* They got the point.'

The men talked politics for a moment. 'Ten bombs across Havana timed to go off when that song played on the radio. No one wants to say Batista's army was defeated badly, but they were. Had their lunch handed to them.' Jack whispered confidentially, 'People are nervous.'

More drinks had been served, Jack had lit a Macanudo, and the conversation had turned suddenly to America. Throughout the wandering discussion, Jack dominated with loud opinions on American interests and the Cuban identity. 'It's a country that can't shake off the paralyzing influence of the mob and Las Vegas. Let's go to a show. We'll all go and we'll feel better. You need to see it to write about it.'

Mueller saw Liz had sunk into the sofa, morose and quiet, and waved off her husband's gamy cigar smoke. She took a small, colorful paper napkin and absentmindedly folded it in halves, quarters, and eighths. Suddenly she turned the full force of her attention to the photographer who sat opposite and was a patient witness to the reunion.

'So you've met,' Liz said, catching Mueller's eyes. 'I'm glad. Katie is a fantastic photographer. She'll be perfect for you. She's done advertising and now she wants to do life. She got that photograph of the married mobster coming out of the Capri with his girlfriend that the New York tabloids made front-page news.'

'Now she's famous,' Jack said.

Katie smiled. 'I'm too busy to be famous.'

'That's a good line,' Jack said. 'Who'd you get it from?'

Liz looked at Mueller. 'So, you've hired her. You won't be disappointed. I've known Katie forever. Since college. God, that feels like forever. She's always been the ambitious one.'

Mueller looked at Katie. 'We'll give it a try.'

Jack had his scotch refilled by one of the vigilant waiters who came off a rank of servers standing at the ready by the bar. Smiling men working hard to mask contempt and all alike in white shirts, black pants, and garroting bow ties. Jack looked right at Mueller. 'Frank Pryce. Know him? He asked a lot of questions. Wanted to know if you were a stand-up guy.'

'What's a stand-up guy?'

'Why would he think you weren't one?'

'Who?' This from Liz.

'George,' Jack said. 'I'm talking about George.'

Mueller paused. 'I think I was in his face.'

Jack mocked. 'You, George, in someone's face?'

'What happened?' Liz asked.

'George has made an enemy here. Didn't take you long, did it? He said you were waiting in El Floridita. The whole thing happened in the rainstorm. You were there to meet a man.'

Mueller raised an eyebrow.

Jack leaned forward. 'You were there asking about a man named Graham. Toby Graham.'

Liz was suddenly alert. 'Who?' She looked at Mueller with strange, wide eyes.

'Graham,' Jack said offhandedly. 'His name is Toby Graham.' He looked at his wife. 'Do you know him?'

Color had left Liz's cheeks and the pallor of sudden surprise gradually faded.

Jack stared at his wife for a moment, but when she didn't answer he addressed Mueller. 'You were asking questions about him.'

'An old acquaintance,' Mueller said. 'Like you, Jack. A year before us. Skull and Bones.' Mueller looked at Liz, who gazed back, taking in everything he'd said, and Mueller paused in thought. He saw Liz take in the name and he saw she'd been startled, as if a dead man had been resurrected.

'You know him?' Jack asked again.

'I can't imagine I do,' Liz whispered. She slumped in the sofa, gave a bright, vacant look of apology, leaned forward again, uncomfortable, and commenced to carelessly flip pages of the portfolio that lay open on the coffee table.

Jack brooked Liz's behavior, but he wasn't oblivious to his wife's sudden distraction, for he looked directly at Mueller, who felt the attention, and he met Jack's eyes. Jack nodded at his wife. 'She's under the weather.'

Liz stood. She walked toward the French doors that opened to the gardens. Jack rose to follow her, but he paused and turned to Mueller. 'Glad you're safe, George. Friday night. The Sans Souci. Join us.'

Mueller had always thought Jack and Liz had a complicated, but durable marriage. He'd always been a stray to them, whom they took in on weekends in Washington DC, when they'd lived in the same city, or they'd had him over for a midweek meal. As a marital entity, they had performed for him. They asked each other's questions and put up a polite wall around who they were as individuals. Mueller had always been amused by how they pretended to have his best interests at heart when they tried to hook him up with blind dates. Polite dinner conversation on modern art or Washington's ugly politics, or religion, were just a distraction from the task of finding him a suitable companion.

To have been intimate with Katie Laurent had been a pleasure, but mostly it had been a mistake. Liz insisted they meet, so he felt he had to go through with the evening, and with dinner came her endless questions that passed for conversation. Katie surprised him when she said her wedding ring was a defense against clients' unwanted advances, and then she removed the ring, and that was the start of her seduction. The next morning, he said they should put their night of tropical besottedness behind them and stick to a professional relationship. They both seemed to know that they would make better colleagues than lovers. She'd given him what she thought he expected of a freelance photographer – and done with the sex they could relax and get on with the work. He found her appealing in the odd way of his complicated cycle of want – not wanting her, getting her, and then, to his surprise, wanting her. What fascinated him was her ambition. He knew that a romance would not end well.

Katie watched Liz leave, and she watched Jack try to catch up. She confided to Mueller, 'I think he's cheating on her.'

'Who?'

'I don't know her name. She's a dancer at the Sans Souci.'

'Jack?'

'Yes, Jack. I am talking about Jack.'

Later, back at his hotel room, Mueller cleaned his head wound with peroxide and dabbed it dry. He saw in his reflection the angry cut that had shocked Liz and in the moment, he chastised himself for thinking he could make a difference. The country has to burn a little.

Mueller again tried to reach Graham on the telephone. It was his third try. The number he had, the one he had called for their one conversation, rang and rang. He called again, careful to dial correctly, and he got the same endless ringing. Each ring went off in his mind like an alarm. He looked at the receiver in his hand and then set it down in its black cradle, perplexed.

4

A BODY APPEARS

THE SWIMMING POOL ON the grounds of the Hotel Capri was more like a pond than the crystal blue pool set against a tableau of sunbathers that appeared on the hotel's promotional brochure. A pond in the shape of a turtle made of tiny azure glass tiles. The body was near the deep end where a mature algarrobo tree cast its cooling shadow.

'Is it a porpoise?'

Mueller had heard that remark in Frank Pryce's summary of the police interviews among surprised hotel guests who had come down for a morning swim and seen the floating object.

Pryce's call had roused Mueller from bed and he'd gotten him to come over by taxi for a chat, but Mueller knew very well that Pryce's use of the word 'chat' was code for something more serious. There was still the requirement that they cooperate, but after the incident in El Floridita, it was less clear how they would succeed. On the way over in the taxi it occurred to

Mueller that under the guise of a chat Pryce intended to scold Mueller for not informing him he was meeting Graham, and perhaps he was going to be dressed down for his uncooperative attitude. There was no point in avoiding Pryce. Sooner or later they'd have to establish a working relationship.

'That's it,' Pryce said to Mueller, pointing. They were together poolside at the opposite end, away from the crowd. Pryce recounted how the pool keeper had looked in the direction of the gray, bloated object and reassured the startled woman who'd asked the question.

'Funny,' Pryce had said to Mueller, 'if it weren't so absurd. How could a porpoise get into a pool a quarter mile from the ocean?'

Summer heat was melting the blacktop on the edge of the patio where they stood away from the water. The bright sun blinded him and washed color from the cabanas. Mueller saw pink shrimp bodies of hotel guests crowded around the pool area as the sun burned down on the bloated object, human only in the clothing that had swollen.

'It's a man,' another woman among the crowd called out energetically, and once she'd made that declaration other hotel guests arriving for their morning swim convened for the best view, attracted and repelled.

Pryce smiled. 'Sorry to get you here on such short notice.' He nodded at the SIM officer whose back was to them. 'Captain Alonzo wanted you here.'

Mueller listened to Pryce report how the body had been discovered, and he was surprised by Pryce's casual manner. He seemed to go on longer than needed, as if he were waiting for Mueller to react, or interrupt, but then Pryce got to the point of their little chat. Pryce nodded again at Captain Alonzo. 'He thinks it might be Toby Graham.'

Mueller was surprised by the way Pryce said it, almost smugly.

'Graham?'

'Yes, Toby Graham. I'm as surprised as you.'

'He suspects or he knows?'

'If he were certain he would have said so. He said he thinks it's him. The body is beyond recognition. It's been dead a couple of days. Probably killed after all the bombs. Too bad you didn't meet him in the bar.'

Mueller ignored the comment. *Graham dead?* Mueller pondered the turn of events and then realized that Pryce was speaking again.

'Captain Alonzo thought you might want to take a look and see if there is something – his shoes perhaps, or a ring – that you might recognize.'

A great queasiness arose in Mueller. He had seen frozen, starved bodies along the Danube in the bitter winter of '48, and there were gunshot victims too, but he'd never gotten over his reluctance to look into the face of death. 'Sure.'

Mueller could already feel the uncertainty of what lay ahead as they approached. It was one thing to see the corpse of a stranger, but the death of an acquaintance made it hard to avoid his uncomfortable feelings about the end of life.

Pryce added, 'We don't have much to go on. If we are to understand this discovery of a body dumped in a hotel pool during the night, and it's clear that he's been dead a couple of days, we need to clarify certain things, such as whether or not it's Toby Graham.'

Mueller found it an odd statement. 'You don't agree with them?' Mueller nodded at Captain Alonzo. Mueller again looked at the man whose back was to them. He was a wiry

43

man in starched tan uniform who stood perfectly still, hands clasped behind his back, and watched his men work to recover the body.

'He would like to believe it is Graham,' Pryce said.

Policemen had taken the long pole used to clean the pool bottom and used the brush end to hook an arm and pull the floating corpse poolside. It took three men to coordinate the movement because the brush end lost purchase and the gray, bloated corpse drifted back to the center. A second pole was brought to the operation and the combined effort of one policeman pulling, the other pushing, succeeded in getting it to a spot where it was tied down like a runaway barge. No one seemed to want to touch the body, but then Captain Alonzo ordered a man to search the pockets, a procedure that required the corpse to be rolled over. Mueller saw the exit wound on the back of the head, where the skull had exploded and brain matter was missing.

'A leather wallet was found in the bottom,' Pryce said. 'Probably thrown in by whoever dumped the body. It was stripped of cash and identification, but there was a photo of a girl. She was blond and the photo was taken against the backdrop of the Washington Monument. And this.'

Mueller looked at a letter written in neat script. Immersion in the pool had made the ink run, but there were enough legible words to see it was written in English.

'So, they think he's American. I checked with the embassy to see if anyone had been reported missing. The police checked their records of the last few days. No one. Nothing. Nada. So you see where I'm going. It's a mystery locked in a puzzle inside a crypt.'

Mueller stared at Pryce. 'The evidence they have to make

them think it's Graham is that they can't identify the body as someone else?'

'Can you tell me where Graham is?' Pryce snapped.

Mueller looked at Pryce. 'No. I can't.' Mueller looked down at the floating corpse, which had righted. The distended cheeks and wide eyes were vaguely human. 'But this is not him.'

'You're sure?'

'Am I sure? No.' Mueller saw Pryce's skepticism. 'Toby Graham is shorter than me. This man is my height. I don't know what happens to a body when it deteriorates. Does it stretch, get taller? I don't know. But I wouldn't start with the presumption that it's Toby Graham just because you don't know who else it might be. Dead American. No identification. That makes it Toby Graham? Sounds like wishful thinking.'

Mueller turned and walked off. He stopped. 'Is this the best these guys can do?'

*

In the taxi on his way back to his hotel. Mueller was certain the body was not Graham, although his certainty was more an act of faith than force of fact. As he drove through Old Havana, eyes catching the waking city coming alive, a thought came to him. There were times when your past catches up with you, and he wondered if that's what had happened here – if it was indeed Toby Graham and his violent past had caught up with him. The thought lingered and was a fitting epitaph to the contradictory threads of Graham's life. The logic of the language – time catching up – the implied moral principle that in the end you are the sum of your actions, was a satisfying notion, but still, Toby Graham dead? That was hard to believe. Graham was too smart, too clever, too prescient to be a hapless gunshot victim found floating in a swimming pool.

The day was young when Mueller got back to his room. There was nothing to do until noon when Katie would drop by for their first excursion to photograph the city. Mueller used the time to draft his first impressions of Cuba. *Holiday* had paid for his trip and it would be bad form to take the money and not deliver an article.

'The story of Havana is hard to decipher,' he wrote his editor, setting himself a tone that would infuse some tolerable truth to the piece, 'even for people who have spent years here, but especially for the visitor who's just arrived. Havana is a city in transition, busily trying to assert itself. The old city by the harbor has colonial churches, dark alleys, and fortress defenses left over from pirate attacks. The smart western districts of Vedado and Miramar have modern glass edifices and Cadillacs, and the local boast is that there are more here per capita than in Miami. And more police. Police everywhere. Comparisons here are all to the neighbor to the north, which is admired, excoriated, or dismissed, but it is always there in any conversation. And Spain too is here, not only in the language and the churches, but the guitars, the colorful clothing, and the easy Latin moods. It's a blithe city, carefree and fun, and you see that in the bars, the lively commerce, the music, and everywhere you see billboards promoting packaged goods, declaring prosperity to people who walk barefoot. It is a young country bursting with ambition, but it hasn't yet found itself as a nation. It seems Cuba's principal business is selling itself to Americans – its sugar, its rum, its beaches, its women. In Havana, anything is possible. That's the line the taxi drivers use when they grab you at the airport and drive you ten miles to your hotel for a scandalous fare. They use the phrase like a proud trophy. White sand beaches, live sex on stage, razzle-dazzle casino gambling. I haven't done any of it yet. We'll see what I get to. And now to those attractions you can add car bombings. Ten in one afternoon. But the attacks haven't closed any of the popular clubs, and police – swarms of police – are there in an instant to roundup suspects, replace sandbags, and collect the sheeted dead.'

Mueller added, 'The little stink of a few rebels traipsing around the Sierra Maestra hasn't driven off the intrepid tourist who booked his room months ago. The message of the city is clear. We are open for business.'

Mueller drafted a letter to the director. There wasn't much to report, setting aside his own arrest, which he didn't want to explain, so he gave an account of his arrival, his several meetings with Pryce, and then, knowing it would interest the director, he said he'd gotten into the swing of the work. He knew it was better to communicate often, even if there wasn't much to report, or much he chose to report, because a lack of news had the potential to turn the director's imagination into an adversary.

But looking over what he'd written he saw that he had unintentionally misled the director. He hadn't mentioned that Graham was missing. He'd written, without context, that Graham was the type of agent who was capable of faking his death as a way to cleanse the scent from his trail.

*

Mueller found Katie in the Nacional's lobby impatiently pointing at her wristwatch. They made up for his being late and spent the day taking photographs, moving about the city looking for its truth – its faces, its poverty, its seductions. Mueller noticed how she got portraits without the subject knowing, and her stamina impressed him, as did the clever way she disguised herself in floppy straw hat, sandals, and baggy shirts so her hidden sex allowed her to move unnoticed among boisterous Cuban men who slapped dominos down at each turn of play. They entered a poor neighborhood near the Central Railway Station and moved from the busy boulevard into a maze of dark alleys filled with smells and loitering men. This was the other Havana, with its poor, its rhythms, its colors, where the white tourist face was an uncommon sight. *In here,* she'd said. Hostile eyes in dark doorways followed them as they walked and everywhere menace stirred.

The silver body of her Leica drew the attention of a barefoot child who called to have his photograph taken. His dirty faced glowed, *Look at me.* Katie ignored Mueller's caution and had the skinny green-eyed boy pose with a defiant face at the sewer's edge – a child with a surly expression. Older boys gathered and surrounded the scene and offered hammy poses, pleading to have their pictures taken. And when she complied they demanded to be paid, hands out, palms greedy. She waved off their request and their eyes were suddenly alive and threatening. Mueller saw it happen all at once – the stones gathered, arms raised – and they found themselves escaping down the alley with angry men in pursuit.

She kept a cool, shrewd smile throughout. He'd reluctantly followed her into the alley with her reassurance that she'd been there before – a lie, he realized when she lost her way. He came to understand her insolence, her daredevil ambition, and he became convinced of her incurably dishonest nature. It made no difference to him. It was hard to carry resentment against a lively, forthright woman who openly used flattery as a tool of persuasion. He saw all this as he walked at her side and watched her snap photographs.

Night followed day with a growing familiarity between them, and the buzz of midday street markets slowly became the exotic steamy feel of evening. They saw the promise of excitement in bars where coy Cuban women huddled with other women and drew the restless gaze of American sailors. And everywhere the closeness of couples walking along El Paseo del Prado oblivious to vigilant police at street corners. Everywhere spontaneous laughter, sirens, and sullen lovers in the heat of the night.

They hadn't planned to go to his hotel room. They found themselves tempted by the idea that they were more interesting and spontaneous than the physics of a professional calculation. They read risk in each other's faces in the elevator. The room was dark when he opened the door and they left it that way so light wouldn't cleanse the mood. In the dark they could be dirty. Passion's talons were planted. She undid her blouse, fumbled with her bra, tossed shoes, and watched him strip down to socks. Moonlight glistened on their pale, naked bodies and they came together in a wordless embrace, cooled by the open balcony's breeze. Her hand clasped his neck, her other hand held his to her breast, lips on lips, and they stumbled to the bed, kissing eyes and nose, and then they collapsed together, laughing.

He was up early the next morning. Wind chimes from the hotel's garden drifted in the balcony's French doors and gladdened the room's silence. Sunlight pouring through the slatted blinds cast banded shadows on the unmade bed.

He thought Katie was pretending sleep, but when he drew close he saw her eyes calm, her mouth parted slightly, breathing lightly. She had turned onto her stomach and cast off the top cotton sheet so her arms lay at her side. Her body had pale sculpted modesty. She was a statue to gaze upon that he knew he could never possess. Yes, the first time they'd been intimate had been a mistake. *Now what?*

Mueller had returned to his journal. He added to his observations to his editor – pondering how to include the phrase, 'that great worm of an island,' which had stuck in his mind ever since the editor had used it.

'What are you writing?'

Her voice startled him. She was sitting up in bed and had pulled the sheet to cover her breasts. Her eyes were wide and curious. He had the impression she had been observing him for some time.

'You're so preoccupied. Writing. Writing. Where did you go?' She had confused him. 'I woke up and you were gone. I went back to sleep.'

Police had called early and asked to see him in the lobby with a few questions to add to the ones he'd answered the day before. Mueller considered a lie. 'The police found a body in a hotel pool. They thought I might know something. Coffee?'

She shook her head, eyes narrow, and then she shrugged her change of heart. 'Sure. I don't care where you were. None of my business. What body?'

'An American, they think.'

She rose jauntily from the bed and wrapped her body in the hotel's terry cloth bathrobe. She looked for a cigarette, but crumpled the cellophane package when she found it empty. She threw the package at him and he shifted in his chair so the hostile projectile sailed harmlessly past. She approached him and sat on his lap. She took his face in her hands so they faced each other and she touched her nose to his. She impaled him with her eyes.

'What?' he asked.

'What are you thinking? I saw you looking at me like that.'

'Like what?'

'Like what am I doing here?'

'I've never met anyone like you. Untamable.'

She laughed hilariously. 'You say the most stupid things. It's hard to know what's really on your mind.' She glanced down at the open journal that he'd covered with his hand. 'About me? No, it wouldn't be about me. I don't think I'm even in your mind.'

He removed his hand. 'Read it.'

She read a few lines, enough to confirm her suspicion, and then she evaluated him like a painter studying a model.

'Hungry?' he asked. He saw he'd confused her. 'Room service? Restaurant?'

'What time is it?'

'Before noon.'

'Okay.'

'Okay which?'

'You choose. I'll shower. Liz warned me you were hard to read. I saw you look at her the other day in the hotel when she first caught your eye. I swear you had the look of a –' She stopped herself, searching for the right word. 'Your expression was vulnerable. I saw this real person. I thought, hell, who is he? Liz said the two of you once had a fling.'

Mueller gave the story – a reluctant sketch of two friends with too much alcohol at a holiday party who found themselves crossing a line. He knew Liz would confirm the facts, or had already offered them, so he felt an obligation to be honest. He

51

had only to provide the additional detail that it had happened *before* Liz married Jack.

'She's concerned about you,' Katie said. 'She doesn't know why you've come to Cuba. She's happy to see you. I think she's worried you're still smitten.'

'That why she set us up?'

Katie shrugged. 'She wants you to be happy.' She looked directly at him. 'This is pleasant – you're fun. We'll look back at this little interlude and laugh. She knows you can help my career.'

Katie's eyes sparkled. 'So gloomy. So much on your mind.' She nodded at the notebook. 'Too busy to be happy.'

Mueller had an impulse to laugh, but instead he stopped her mouth with a kiss that she returned with surprising ardor.

Suddenly she pulled back. She tweaked his nose. *'Busy. Busy.'* She hopped off his lap and began a stretch routine on the floor, rolling her head side to side, and then pulling each elbow forward to release shoulder tension. She bent over straight knees and placed her palms on the floor.

It took him a moment to realize that she had forgotten about him.

5

RESURRECTION

Surprise is a funny thing. It's quickly lost in the rush of thoughts that follow the sudden and the unexpected – and that is what happened to Mueller when he opened an envelope that he found slipped under his hotel room door. Graham's note gave a time and a place to meet.

'Meet him, of course,' Pryce said.

Mueller had gone to the embassy to show Pryce the note. An olive branch. An air-conditioned room on an upper floor, plain and empty. No windows. No natural light. No sense of time. Only a brace of limp flags and the vapid portraits of two heads of state.

'You knew it wasn't Graham in the pool,' Mueller snapped. 'Why did you mislead me?' The question upended the moment. Mueller was irritated that the whole affair was becoming a grotesque soap opera in which he was a reluctant player with a bit part.

Pryce's bushy eyebrows arched. 'Of course, it wasn't. Alonzo suggested it. I went along. It was helpful to see if you bought the story. You were uncertain so I knew you weren't collaborating against me. After the incident in the bar I wanted to know if I was being played.' Pryce folded his hands and gazed solemnly. 'I don't want to be a patsy to the misguided intentions of a hotshot and his brainy fool friend.'

Mueller smiled at the insult. Self-deprecation was a strategy too. He knew better than to allow spite to jeopardize a deceit. 'Well, then we've got that settled, haven't we?'

'Settled?'

'We know where we stand. We distrust each other. That will make it easier to work together.'

Pryce took a moment to laugh. 'I like you, George. I like your sense of humor. Dry like ice.' Pryce leaned back in his chair, exciting a crack in the joinery, and then came forward toward Mueller. 'You'll appreciate this.' He pushed the morning's English-language newspaper across the table.

Mueller saw the headline: 'Capitalist Pigs.' He read how rebels of the July 26th Movement had released a dozen hogs in the Sans Souci casino during a crowded floor show. Pandemonium ensued.

'Someone's idea of a joke,' Pryce said.

'The headline or the incident?'

'Both,' Pryce said. 'Batista tortures children. Rebels stage political theater. Humor, George, a tactical weapon in the battle for hearts and minds. Bombs help. And rifles.'

Mueller pondered what point he was making. He pushed the newspaper back across the table. 'And?'

'There is no and. It's easy to be sympathetic to the rebels. That's the point.'

Mueller looked at Pryce. There was a beat of silence.

'Are you?'

Mueller allowed himself to smile. 'Is that what this is about?'

'Let me show you something.'

They left the embassy together. It was near midnight. This was Frank Pryce. Newly appointed FBI attaché serving the ambassador and making a name for himself with long hours. He took up his position in Havana at the request of the head of the FBI, accepting a lower post, but a sensitive one, to become a trusting set of eyes and ears for certain powerful men in Washington. And there was more Mueller had gotten from Lockwood. Pryce made a name for himself in the FBI's antimob campaigns, leading investigations into corrupt gambling in Nevada, getting his picture in the newspaper when he made surprise arrests. He epitomized the FBI's cop mentality and its rigid policing, and he was of that early generation of government agent who thought himself incorruptible. He was good at making arrests, but not so good at playing out cases for the longer view of counterintelligence. Three years before, he'd moved inexplicably to the FBI's operations in Mexico when it was one of the few overseas operations the FBI was allowed to retain after the CIA took over in Costa Rica, Honduras, Haiti, Brazil, and Venezuela. He committed a bureaucratic act of war in Caracas, destroying files, rolling up networks, and abandoning cases, before turning the office over to the CIA. Mueller's soundings on Pryce, from Lockwood and his own sources, were mixed at best. 'Bagman for the top man, but a quick study. Carries a copy of the Constitution.' And from a State Department G-15, who was in a position to know: 'Very cooperative when he needs to be.' *And when he doesn't?* 'Well, he can be a poke in the eye. It's all about the law. Being on one side of it.'

A taxi dropped them at a dark alley in Old Havana that curved past the colonial Custom House. Cobblestones in the street were bisected by an open channel, wide and foul, and as it was dimly lit, they didn't know if the smell was waste or death. In the dark, there was laughter, music, and loud voices that erupted from suddenly opened doors and then silenced when the doors slammed shut. Two Americans stumbled from a bar boisterous and exuberant with drink, making horrible uncouth sounds, howling and wailing in the night, pretending to box. The pretense vanished when an insult begat injury, and playful slapping got violent.

Pryce groaned his disgust. Taking Mueller's arm, he led him farther into the alley's darkness, toward the harbor, and as they rounded one corner, the sounds of conflict grew faint and Mueller felt a great silence around them, pierced only by the quickening pace of their footsteps.

'In here,' Pryce said.

They had arrived at a stone façade of arched openings faced with iron grates from which cool air flowed into the torpid evening. The warehouse brooded in amber light cast by a single street lamp. It was located with obvious logic facing the narrow harbor channel and the jutting quay, deserted at that late hour except for a restless dog moving in the shadows and a cream-colored Packard sedan with chrome trim. The driver sat in the dark.

Mueller followed Pryce through a doorway and found himself in a large space with a ceiling of skylights. Moonlight provided illumination to look around and gauge the emptiness of the place. A forklift held the center of the room with its quiet, monumental coldness. Before it, like an offering, a pallet that held a long rectangular crate, its coarse surface a crude wooden sarcophagus. Mueller felt the presence of a third man before he heard footsteps. A door had opened, closed, and a short, thin man approached from the darkness. He was swarthy but dressed in white – pale skinny tie, ivory suit, and cream shoes. The only color was a crimson pocket square. He carried a black crowbar in his hands, and his eyes were unkind.

'This is Mickey Ruden. Open it,' he instructed.

A great aching screech of nails pulled from unyielding wood came when the crowbar pried the lid, which came off with the ease of a thing that had been opened before. Ruden dropped the crowbar to the concrete floor and the clang reverberated in the warehouse.

Mueller saw the guns. New M1 Garand rifles packed in protective oilskin. Pryce handed one to Mueller, who refused it. What was the point of holding a rifle? He was uncomfortable in the presence of embargoed goods.

'He found them on a fishing boat in the harbor. They came from a DC-3 that landed near Nuevitas. His guys got a tip from the harbor master. They were stolen from an arms depot at Fort Rucker in Alabama then sold into the international arms market, bought in Vienna, and shipped here. No one filed off the serial numbers.' Pryce raised his eyebrow. 'It's just the sort of thing you'd expect from the CIA.' He waved deeper into the warehouse where there was a second crate. 'One hundred rifles.'

Mueller let himself be led a few steps away so they could speak without being overheard. Pryce went on with his speculation in a voice that shifted, probed, threatened, and cajoled, pressing Mueller on what he was doing in Cuba, his imperturbability showing flashes of irritation. Why had he come down? 'You expect me to believe what they said?'

Then Pryce pounced. 'There are rumors, George. Batista came

to power in an army coup and he'll leave the way he entered. He surrounds himself with incompetent army loyalists and he's promoted inept officers who don't know how to do their jobs. He's pushed aside career air force officers he doesn't trust. He takes from the National Lottery and makes lavish gifts to the Roman Catholic Church, newspapermen, and American politicians. The stink of corruption is suffocating this country.'

Pryce nodded at the hoodlum and lowered his voice. 'The Havana mob is worried. They wouldn't bring me this evidence if they weren't worried. They have a good business here. Batista is reliably corrupt. The air force is not.'

Pryce paused again to make sure Mueller understood. The two men were the same height, but Mueller had an ascetic thinness and Pryce was a big man with threatening bulk. The two men were made to appear small and intimate standing a few feet apart in the vast empty space.

Mueller pointed at the crate and snapped, 'If the CIA was going to arm a coup they wouldn't send down a crate of rifles.' Mueller stopped Pryce's protest with conviction in his voice. 'Graham is capable of many things, but not incompetence. A crate of rifles? Cuba is a warren of predators looking to see who will eat, or be eaten. Fear all, trust few, be kind to none. Do your job, Frank. Don't get lost in byzantine speculation.'

Pryce nodded at the mobster holding the crowbar. He looked again at Mueller. 'All good points. If you're right, George, and you seem to think you're right, and I'll grant the logic of your observations, tell me so I understand, who would want me to believe the CIA was behind a coup?'

'I'm the amateur, remember. The guy who can't get his tradecraft right.'

Scorn and disdain accompanied Pryce's smile. 'Be careful,

George. I'm not the only one asking questions. Bodies appear in swimming pools. That's how things are done here.'

*

It was eleven o'clock in the morning when Mueller, having been awake for twenty minutes thinking about the evening's events, as if going over a dream, finally opened his eyes. Sunlight flushed shy thoughts from his mind. He turned to his right, thinking Katie was in bed, but she was not, and he realized she too had been in his dream. He stood and approached the hotel room desk in his underwear. There, where he'd left them, were the careful notes he had made for the telex he'd sent to the director before going to bed.

The notes were a reminder that he'd done some hard thinking the night before trying to make sense of Pryce's show and tell. He'd mocked Pryce's theory, not because he believed his ridicule, but because he thought it was best to reject the suggestion until he had the facts. Helpful lies, disguising truths. Mueller felt in Pryce the gravitational pull of a calculating intelligence. He was prepared to respect the danger he posed even if he wasn't prepared to like the man. Mueller felt in that part of his mind that calibrates threats before they are obvious the risk of being made complicit in a crime.

That the mob was cooperating with Pryce should have been a clue, but he couldn't believe that a man of Pryce's rigid character would allow himself to be knowingly used. The answer, he thought, was to see everything about Pryce through the prism of his heartfelt policing. Arms brought in. Embargo breached. The law broken. He was a cop. His job was to make an arrest. Pryce gave cursory thought to the question that most interested

Mueller. Incompetence resulted in an easy interdiction. Who benefited from exposure of the amateur effort?

Mueller had kept to the facts in his telex to the director, but even what he thought passed for fact was really only tentative observation about a bizarre opera. He kept thinking of himself as offstage waiting to step out and sing his part.

He again read the director's response. It had been delivered before nine o'clock when he was abruptly awoken by the concierge, and after reading it half asleep he'd put it aside and gone back to bed. Now, with it in his hands again, he puzzled over the paragraph. 'Dear George,' it began.

Dear George? When had the director ever started a correspondence as a personal letter? That false note had stopped Mueller on his first reading, and being less than awake he'd put the letter aside until he could fathom the dissembling implications of the endearment. Mueller found the director's note baffling.

'I suppose we should be flattered. If I thought there was anyone who was a good candidate, worth propping up, we'd do it. I don't have qualms about that. But the whole tomato is rotten. Generals who aren't loyal to the president are loyal to their greed. We have no good options. But still it's good to know that we're viewed as the chess master who would try that gambit. Let Pryce believe the story if he wants to believe it. It will keep him busy.'

Then, 'We checked on the guy Ruden. Owns two casinos. Clever like a fox. He can fall asleep in the middle of a meeting and wake up at precisely the right moment and join the conversation completely coherent. The New York DA wants him for questioning in the murder of a mobster in Long Island. Shot the man in both cheeks and then in the back of the head. How are you getting along? How's Graham?'

6

WAITING REDUX

MUELLER SAT IN THE booth in El Floridita with a mordant sense of déjà vu. Same seat. Same table, being served by the same waiter. Graham was late again.

Mueller knew the place now – the drink menu, the sullen waiter who waited impatiently for Mueller to place a drink order, the tinny radio playing 'Volare.' The song was everywhere. The plate-glass window was replaced, but the bar's name had not been stenciled in gold yet, and a fresh coat of paint covered the wall that had been splattered with the woman's blood.

The obvious hit Mueller. He leapt to a conclusion – but that was what he was trained to do. And he constructed in his mind a summary of what he'd come to think – speculate really – and he repeated it, testing the proposition. Could it be true? A thirty-seven-year-old CIA officer once earmarked for great things was engaged in an act of deception so outrageous that if attributed to him it would be viewed as an act of insubordination that would cost him his career and possibly his life: namely, delivering embargoed weapons to the opposition to provoke rumors of a coup d'état. Who gained from this?

Suddenly, Toby Graham slipped into the booth opposite Mueller. The two men took each other in. 'Good to see you, George. Here we are. Finally.'

'Good to see you're alive.'

Graham nodded, smiled. 'Staying ahead of the Grim Reaper. My specialty.'

Mueller saw in Graham's darting eyes a cautious man in a public bar acutely aware of his surroundings. He watched Graham take in the few tourists who braved the target the bar had become. He thought Graham had aged, his face thinned and his trademark cockiness frayed.

Graham leaned forward and whispered. 'You look lost in thought. Just like the old George. Always a thinker.'

'You're still good for a surprise.'

'Keeps things lively. Boredom is the enemy here.'

Mueller accounted for his first memory of the unexpected in Graham. It was in a literature survey course taught by a pigheaded professor, himself a graduate of the college, who valued in equal measure classroom decorum and bright minds. Graham's disrespectful correction of the professor's comment on *The Merchant of Venice* had caught Mueller's attention. Graham showed himself to be well-spoken, and he'd actually read the play, which Mueller had not. He was nimble with words, had easy charm and fit physique, which taken as a whole, made him seem destined for greatness. His careless attention to clothing, the relaxed fit of his trousers, and the way he always seemed to look good in whatever he wore were details Mueller had noticed. If Mueller had allowed himself to think the thought he would have admitted he was attracted to Graham – his confidence, his cleverness, his smile. Now, he dressed the part of a local. Sandals, blousy *guayabara* shirt, and a green-banded straw fedora so he could pass for a Cuban.

'You've gotten sloppy, George.' Graham nodded at a table across the room. 'The man there, sipping his coffee. He followed you. Your effort to help the girl was noble and heroic, but now you're a person of interest.'

'It's not because I'm here with you.'

Graham smiled. 'Alonzo has his eye on both of us.' Graham looked directly at Mueller. 'So, George, what brought you down? How did they get you out of retirement? Don't expect me to believe that cock and bull story you're writing a travel piece. Don't impeach my trust with a lie.'

'They're worried about you.'

'Worried? So they sent you down to reassure them. Tell them not to worry. Worried about what?'

'Following the playbook. Isn't that what it's always about?'

'What it's always about is never what it's about. You know that. Or have you forgotten? The right hand does one thing, the left hand another, and the two men to whom those hands belong talk out of both sides of their mouth. There is only one thing clear here.'

Graham pointed out the window at the gleaming cupola of the Presidential Palace, which peeked above Beaux Arts apartments along El Paseo del Prado. 'Dante divided his hell into nine circles. He put the criminals in the seventh circle, thieves in the eighth, and traitors in the ninth. When the devil has to pick a circle for Batista he will have a difficult choice. Batista is a *monstrum horrendum*.' Graham's eyes sparkled. 'But he is *our monstrum horrendum*.'

Mueller didn't hear a trace of irony in Graham's voice. Graham added, 'Tell them that things are falling apart. They won't want to hear that, but the director might believe it if he hears it from you. No one in Headquarters wants to believe that Batista will fall.'

'Is it imminent?'

'Imminent?' Graham laughed. 'The whole damned country is about to blow up. Yes, I'd say it was imminent.'

Graham paused and spoke circumspectly. 'Lockwood was down here last week. Surprise visit. I joined him with the ambassador to meet Batista. Protocol visit. The ambassador's limousine with its American flags on the front bumpers drove us past the barbed-wire barricade guarded by soldiers with tommy guns. We went in the rear entrance to make it easier for his wheelchair. Batista came out and greeted us. Shook our hands. His English is very good, helped by his previous exile in Miami. He wore his general's uniform and was remarkably calm, collected, and funny. He sent for coffee when we got to his office and he offered Cuban cigars.

'He showed the ambassador his gold telephone, a gift from ITT. Then he showed off a portrait of José Martí that hangs on the wall, and the point of their conversation was that it could be improved if it was lit better. I couldn't believe this was the thing that interested them. Batista brought up Abraham Lincoln, one of his heroes, and he said he hoped history would judge him Cuba's Abraham Lincoln. After coffee and cigars Batista gathered us for a group photograph as a souvenir of the meeting. You know we don't like to have our photos taken, but there we were, Lockwood and me, in his office, and there was no way to avoid the moment. So, he had us. The meeting ended. Nothing was accomplished, no agreement on elections, nothing of substance said. The next day the photograph appeared in the newspapers with the caption: *El Presidente Enjoys the Full Support of the American Ambassador and His Ally, CIA Inspector General Lockwood.'*

Graham paused. 'Batista made himself look good to everyone here who believes the embargo means he's lost support in Washington. Well, George, Washington doesn't have a clue. They are being played.'

Graham's eyes narrowed, his voice deepened, his words had a mocking tone. 'The State Department would have us believe that a third force will emerge around Rivero Aqüero. Here's their scenario. Batista succumbs to pressure of our arms embargo. Elections are held. A new government is formed. Well, George, that won't happen. Rivero Aqüero is a fraud. Batista will hold on, fingers grasping at power, because who among us is ready to willingly give it up?'

Mueller saw Graham's eyes become fervent, the eyes of a man too much in his own mind, too long on a bayonet border, too close to disillusionment. It was something Mueller knew, and in knowing it he recognized it.

'America is a wonderful place,' Graham said, 'but one mistake I don't make, nor should you, if you're thoughtful, and I know you are – more thoughtful than most – is to mistake patriotism for love of country. Chest-thumping patriotism is all the fashion on Capitol Hill. It's a sloppy mix of fear and ignorance worn self-righteously. Patriots embrace freedom and democracy like they are God-given and yet here and in Guatemala – places I've got experience of – those patriots prop up men like Castillo Armas, men like Batista. These eloquent defenders of democracy embrace dictators.'

Graham paused. 'Be careful of Pryce. He doesn't believe, or

refuses to admit, that for every boy Batista kills two more join the rebellion. Dictators fall. They always do. Batista's days are numbered. What does he do? He stands in front of José Martí's portrait and thinks how to improve the lighting. *God dammit*, George, that's what you need to see.'

Mueller wasn't so much disturbed by Graham's outburst as he was startled by it. Every agent in the field was vulnerable to the corrosive effects of the work, and the hypocrisies, but you learned to keep those thoughts to yourself.

Graham grew quiet. He leaned forward. 'How did you do it?'

'Do what?'

'Get out without them making your life miserable.'

Mueller saw something in Graham's eyes he'd never seen before. Was it fear? Mueller looked away. When he turned back he met Graham's gaze. 'They need to believe you are loyal. That you'll keep your mouth shut.'

Mueller glanced at the bar where the Cuban Graham had pointed out continued to quietly observe them, but he looked away when Mueller stared.

Mueller smiled. 'They say Hemingway comes in here.'

'That's what they say. What the owner wants you to believe.'

He nodded at the rank of sailors at the bar. 'Good for business. You know what they say about him. What he would like you to believe. We are all moved by his novels and fascinated by the macho legend he's made of himself. Three daiquiris, yes, but it's a big lie that he's not an alcoholic. He believes the myths about himself. Batista suffers the same way.' Graham looked at Mueller. 'You get your interview with him?'

'No'

'On the phone you said it was a done deal.'

'I thought it was.' Mueller contemplated how much to say. 'I telexed him before I came down. He said come down. Now I can't get him on the phone.'

'He's avoiding you.'

'It would seem so.'

'He probably found out you don't drink. He doesn't like a writer who doesn't drink. He doesn't want a long conversation with a sober man who keeps him from his daiquiris.'

They never did order drinks at El Floridita.

Graham suggested they leave to get away from the undercover policeman. They performed a tradecraft routine they had successfully pulled over in Vienna when they'd wanted to escape an NKVD agent, splitting up, forcing the agent to make a choice, and then the one who'd lost the tail doubled back and created a distracting disturbance for the other. They pulled it off again, and found in their success a measure of boyish camaraderie.

'You've gained a few pounds,' Graham said, throwing himself into a dark door beside a breathless Mueller as they watched their SIM tail run by. 'But you haven't lost the touch. You should get back in the game. Pair up with me.'

Mueller laughed at Graham's sarcasm. He'd gotten that offer once before, a memorable cold night in Vienna, but it was a different circumstance, a different danger, waiting to meet their 'blind date' at the corner of Dorotheergasse and Stallburggasse. It was a good meeting place, at least for the KGB walk-in who'd chosen it – the center of the Innere Stadt, near the Graben, with its statue to the victims of the great plague, and far from any American outposts. She was a pretty Soviet agent and Mueller had taken to her, and he'd let himself believe that she wanted to defect. He'd arrived by tram with her, but on the square, in the open, she had stepped back. Suddenly, Graham had rushed from an alley and gone for the girl, tripping Mueller, who fell, and the sniper's bullet missed. Graham had saved Mueller's life, but he didn't know if it had been inadvertent. He never asked. Graham had done something for him and that created a tie. Was it friendship? He didn't think it was. But there was a tie and with it came a peril.

They stepped from the shadows of the alley free men. The evening was alive. Brassy music drifted from open bars and mixed with the easy laughter of couples strolling in the heavy air of a tropical night, fanning themselves. Mueller was beginning to like Havana, the edgy, adventurous feel of the city, the exotic moods of its people. Habaneros, they called themselves, a people of passion and intellect.

The two men strolled together, each alone in his thoughts, but from time to time the sensual movement of a woman alone among the crowd drew their restless eyes, and everywhere the romantic closeness of couples.

A cleansing sea breeze removed the smell of the city's sewers and mixed with rich aromas of spicy foods on sidewalk tables. One restaurant's advertisement for pork on the menu was a freshly cut hog's head stuck on a spike in the window.

Upon passing the end of one street they came upon a line of women in short skirts, loose tops, and stiletto heels. As Graham passed the line of prostitutes the bold ones blew an air kiss, or motioned with a come-hither finger, and expectant energy charged the air. Graham nodded at one, acknowledging the solicitation, and to Mueller, a half step behind, he said in a whispery baritone, 'The shame of this country is that it hasn't found a way to stop selling itself.'

At one point in their stroll Graham turned onto a leafy street of Beaux Arts homes. They had entered from a broad avenue and were now stopped at an iron gate that opened into a garden. The two-story pink mansion was dark.

'I got it for a bargain,' Graham said. 'I could never afford the rent but the owner is an American executive whose wife was worried about the war. She insisted he be transferred back to Chicago. I got it month-to-month for a pittance. Comes with a maid and gardener.'

It was cool outside, but warm in the second-floor living room even with the French doors open to the balcony. A gentle sea breeze entered, but there was still sticky humidity in the room's confined air.

Graham pulled a bottle of Benedictine from the liquor cabinet hidden within a huge colonial breakfront that dominated a wall.

'What is it?' Mueller asked, taking a glass.

'Taste it. Doesn't matter what it is. It's how it tastes.' Graham poured himself a glass and then he proceeded to strip down to his boxer shorts. He sat at a little ceramic tile table on the balcony, bare legs crossed, naked chest, and sipped his liqueur. 'Monks make it. It cools you off. That's what it does. A pleasant way to end a hot day.' He looked at Mueller. 'To us.'

Mueller lifted his glass. It wasn't how he thought the evening would unfold, to find himself sitting on a balcony under the moonless sky with Graham in his underwear. He wondered if Graham was going to come on to him, but that never happened. Mueller didn't join Graham in his state of undress, nor did he feel any pressure to do so, and he came to think getting down to white boxer shorts was Graham's quirk.

They talked about nothing in particular for an hour, or nothing Mueller could later remember, and the conversation drifted in that way until Mueller said, 'Some people thought you were dead.'

Graham laughed. 'Some people wish I were dead.' Then out of the blue, 'So, George, what brought you down?'

'I thought I answered that.'

'What did you say?'

'They're worried about you.'

'Right. Good to know I'm on their mind. The danger comes when they've forgotten about you.'

Mueller sipped the liqueur in his snifter glass. 'You should be careful of Pryce. But then you already know that, don't you?'

Graham sipped. 'I do. Is there something you know?'

'He thinks you're planning a coup.'

Graham laughed dismissively. 'He doesn't know how to dance.' Graham saw that he had confused Mueller. 'It's more poetic in Spanish. A man who can't dance is dull, flatfooted. Keep your eyes open so he doesn't step on your toes.'

Graham enjoyed the last of his drink. He pointed beyond the balcony to a pale mansion diagonally across the street surrounded by graceful, mature trees. Lights in the second floor were on, a curtain was open, and a naked woman in silhouette was visible.

'Just by coincidence I found myself neighbors to Jack Malone and his wife, Liz. You know her, don't you? Know her well?'

It was the way Graham looked at Mueller that led him to think, as one does when a question comes suddenly and surprises, and is, by its having been asked, something to make one curious, that he realized they'd come to the point of the evening. Later, his memory would summon Graham's question, and he'd ponder the intensity of Graham's curiosity, disguised within the cloaking casualness of an offhand remark.

'Know her? Yes. Know her well? I suppose I do.'

Mueller gave the details of their acquaintance – having met

through Jack. Mueller said there were things he didn't like about Jack, but he respected him for having the good sense to marry someone like Liz to soften his rough edges. Mueller saw Graham listen intensely. The eager listening encouraged Mueller to say more than he intended, describing husband and wife.

'He's a bit of a social bully,' Graham said.

Mueller met Graham's eyes. 'Did you know him in college?'

'No. Different houses. I was on scholarship,' Graham added. 'Liz confided in me.'

'Oh, really.' Knowing that Graham had an established interest in Liz didn't bother Mueller, but it wasn't something he was going to forget.

'Small world,' Graham said. 'Jack called me. He heard you were looking for me and on the pretense that we had some history together, or were from the same college, if that counts as history, he asked me to join a little group he was forming for tomorrow night at the casino.'

7

SANS SOUCI

MUELLER STOOD INSIDE THE Spanish villa entrance and marveled at the Sans Souci's opulence, listening to Jack's exuberant description of all there was. Shiny slot machines lined the wide mosaic tile hall and elegant couples wandered with dazzled eyes.

'It's French,' Jack said. 'Means without care. And if you don't care about losing your shirt you can have a good time gambling. They've got roulette, craps, blackjack, and a poor man's carnival game with eight dice and a board. Players have a one-in-a-thousand chance of winning, but the croupier's job is to convince you otherwise. A Manhattan doctor lost twenty-five thousand last week. It's run by the mob. No one cheats.'

The two men were alone at the base of gracefully curved stone steps that had brought them to a patio with milling drinkers who stood among groomed palms. Prominently in the center was a majestic fountain where crystal water, illuminated by rainbow lights, cascaded level to level. Perfume of tropical flowers infused the hint of brackish waste from beyond the casino's walls. An energetic Afro-Cuban band played a wild Caribbean mambo and a couple moved in quick orchestrated steps. They were obviously from the show – she in flamboyant dress and a flower hat, he an athletic man in tuxedo – and then a dozen men and women from the milling crowd joined in. These tourists dressed in banded straw fedoras, guayabara shirts, and flowery smocks bought in the street to enhance their claim on the spirit of the country. A surplus of waiters hustled among the array of tables, giving energy to the sparse crowd. Long tables radiated out from the stage like spokes on a wheel and each was heaped with bottles of white rum, spiny lobster tails, blackened ham, and beans served over rice.

Mueller sensed a precarious air to the partygoers' carefree liveliness – the possibility that the evening would be suddenly interrupted by a gunshot in the street, or a bomb. Tourists willed themselves into bliss until a wailing siren put an end to the night.

Jack nodded at the stage where two heavyset thugs in suits stood guard. 'That's where the pigs came out. Ten huge hogs. Pandemonium. One woman from Cincinnati had to get a tetanus shot.' Jack waved over the young Cuban woman who had started the evening's dancing. 'Her name is Ofelia. Let me introduce you.'

Jack presented the woman. Her strapless dress swayed at her ankles and her head was crowned with an elaborate nosegay. She was slight, with narrow hips, pearl skin, and raven hair, and had the quality of handmade beauty coveted in the commerce of casino floor shows.

'This is my friend George Mueller.' Then, to Mueller, 'She's a wonderful dancer. She wants to work in Las Vegas, but immigrant visas are tough to get. There is a waiting list. You know people. Maybe you can help.'

Mueller saw her eyes widen hopefully. 'The people I know are gone. I don't know anyone in the embassy.' He put forward his hand to greet her, but lowered his hand when he saw her disappointment. Her eyes impaled his coldly. The awkward moment lingered.

She turned to Jack. 'You are full of empty promises. I must change. The show starts.' Her eyes darted to the shadows of the room and she became agitated. 'We can't speak to customers. Nunca. They see us.' She swung around and headed toward a stage door marked No Entrada.

Jack turned to Mueller, 'Her English is better than you think. We found her in Camaguey and I got her this job.'

'What did you tell her I could do for her?'

'I said you had connections. She'd be grateful for whatever you can do. Tell her you'll ask around. I know it's tough. Do me that favor. Give her some encouragement.'

Jack wrapped his arm around Mueller's shoulder, dismissing the discussion, and smiled broadly. 'Aren't you glad you came?' He waved at the opulence. 'Nothing like this in New Haven. You'd have to go to Paris to get this decadence, but they don't have beaches and no floor shows. Not like this. You'll see.' He pointed to customers gathering at tables. 'It's a good crowd given the bombs. Those men there are the beef buyers I'm entertaining. Good men who fill in their partying with a few hours of work. They came to see the prize steers we're selling. They left their wives and manners at home.'

Jack took a gratis Macanudo from a waiter's open box and grabbed a champagne flute from a passing tray. 'Drink, George.

There's Coca-Cola too. I've never liked its candied sweetness unless it was cut with rum. Come on. Do me the favor.'

Jack pulled Mueller to the stage door and blithely ignored the big yellow sign prohibiting entry. Mueller found himself in a dimly light hallway alive with people clinging to the walls. Half-dressed dancers, men and women, who suddenly stopped talking when the two Americans passed, and then resumed their chatter a moment later. Jack knocked twice lightly on a frosted glass pane of a dressing room, and he pushed the door open before there was a response from inside.

Ofelia sat across the tiny dressing room. She was seated at the large, arched vanity mirror with her back to them, wearing a bra. Before her, a clutter of creams, wigs, perfume, combs, brushes, and a jumble of bras. Mueller saw the back of her head, her black hair loose to her neck, and then he saw her looking directly at him through the reflection. She spun around. 'Que?' She stared at Jack. 'Who is he?'

Mueller almost laughed. Ofelia lifted articles of clothing from the vanity and began throwing them to the floor, looking for one thing, and not finding it, she dropped a scarlet blouse, a flowered shirt, a confining carnelian top, silver rhinestone brassiere, and as she did she swore in an angry soprano, examining one thing, then another. She rejected each and then as suddenly as her search had begun, it stopped. She turned to Mueller. 'I know you. We just met.'

She stood and quickly wrapped herself in a terry cloth bathrobe, pulling the neck line closed. 'I am late. *Todo está desorganizado. Mi vida.* My costume.' Ofelia again stared at Mueller, but this time she looked at him as if trying to see inside his mind.

Mueller thought: *Who is this woman?* Not yet twenty, he

thought. Wild. Insulting. He saw the whole of her life in her pleading eyes. Her smooth hands revealed her privilege. Her fair skin unmasked her age. 'I'll see what I can do,' he said.

A quick gasp of breath spoke her surprise. Her tears gave away her gratitude. She foreswore all callous pretense. Emotion triumphed and broke through in a fragile voice. She kissed his hand. *'Gracias! Gracias!'* Her eyes sparkled.

Jack and Mueller were again in the hall passing the other dancers, who stepped back to let the two men pass.

'What did I agree to?' Mueller asked.

'Nothing,' Jack said. 'She's grateful. That's enough. Immigrant visas are impossible now. You made her feel better. She won't be happy on this island. Her eyes are wide for the world. She wears ambition like a curse.'

*

'We thought we'd lost you,' Katie yelled.

Mueller heard his name called as he stood beside Jack at the cascading fountain. Liz and Katie approached, laughing brightly, each holding a colorful drink. Their exuberance contained Jack's big personality and the women smiled, claiming the moment with mocking eyes.

Katie turned to Jack. 'You look startled to see us.' She poked him with her finger and turned to Mueller. 'This is what you do in Havana. You see the shows. Dancing. Food. Liquor. You won't believe what they do onstage. I had to convince Liz to come. She's not sure she wants to be here.'

Liz smiled unhappily. 'Anything for you. I'm sure I'll tolerate the nudity.'

Mueller nodded. He too had come along with a vague

interest, and he wasn't enthusiastic about being reduced to an American tourist doing the casino circuit. But he was curious, and if he was honest with himself, he wanted to investigate the scandalous offering that lured businessmen on their weeklong junkets without wives. There was always something to learn from buttoned up men letting loose in the safe space of licensed striptease. Jack had called twice to remind him of the invitation. Mueller obliged, thinking that if he got bored, or he found the company tiring, he'd slip away. And he knew that some of what he saw would find its way into his magazine piece – and please the editor – and that thought convinced him.

Jack again put his arm around Mueller and repeated, 'Glad you came?'

The four of them had made their way to a table marked 'Reserved,' and six seats were held for their party. One of the six seats was already occupied.

'Here's someone I thought you'd like to see,' Jack said. Later, Mueller realized he shouldn't have been surprised to see Toby Graham seated at the table. Graham turned, having risen from his seat, and faced Mueller and in the suddenness of his getting up came the surprise.

Mueller felt Jack's fingers dig into his shoulder in the unpleasant way he had of putting physical emphasis on his declarations. Jack boasted. 'I had one hell of a time finding him and it took some persuasion to get him here, but I told him you'd be here and that was enough.'

Jack turned to Graham. 'You know George, of course. Quiet man. Former diplomat. Teaches Shakespeare. Always lost to me at poker. He can't bluff to save his life.'

Jack coaxed Liz forward to join the little group.

Mueller saw Liz's face had the startling pallor of death.

'My wife, Liz. And her friend Katie.' Jack turned to Liz. 'This is the guy George was looking for. Works in the embassy doing something he can't talk about. Is he the guy you thought you didn't know?'

Mueller looked at Jack, curious about the way he phrased his question, as if he were confirming a suspicion.

'We've met,' Liz said. 'Through George.'

Mueller didn't impeach her lie.

Jack added, 'He works in Camaguey.' Jack turned to Graham. 'Community development work. Is that right?'

'Yes.' Graham looked at Liz, who looked away.

'You're near us. Our ranch is an hour north. We'll get you out for a visit.'

The moment was usurped by an explosion of brassy sound from the stage. It was the call to be seated, and the music drove the group to their chairs. Mueller found himself beside Graham and across from Katie, and Liz was on his other side, so he was aware of his place separating them. Jack had gone to the other end and greeted his cattle buyers, pressing fingers into shoulders, making small talk, and when he was done, he sat beside Katie. Jack looked over his spiny lobster tail at Graham.

'There was a rumor you were dead.'

Graham raised an eyebrow. 'In Cuba you discover that things aren't always as they seem. Castro has been reported dead three times and each time he's had a miraculous resurrection.' Graham smiled. 'Here in Cuba death can be a temporary matter.'

'That's a good line,' Jack said. 'Maybe George will put it into his travel piece. How is the piece going? Anything good?'

'Good? Where's your confidence in me?'

'Go to Colon Cemetery. It's bigger than Père Lachaise in

Paris. No one writes about it.' He looked at Graham. 'Nothing temporary about the dead in Colon Cemetery.'

Jack turned his attention to the cattle buyers, and Mueller looked at Liz, and then at Graham. Liz was sullen, eyes on her plate, avoiding the conversation. Graham was quiet too, his eyes fixed on the glass of rum that his fingers touched like a chalice. Mueller looked at each, but neither looked at him, or at each other. Mueller again found himself in Jack's orbit.

'And this too is a fact.'

Mueller had missed the predicate so he leaned closer to understand what had been said, all the while nodding knowingly, because to do otherwise would have been rude.

'She was a new maid at the ranch,' Jack said to the cattle buyers, 'and she knew no English. Not a word. And Liz's Spanish was not too good at the time. We were hosting dinner for the ambassador, the previous one – a nice fellow but a political appointment who had no clue about Cuba and didn't speak Spanish – and his wife. Liz wanted everything to be perfect for our guests. She told the maid that she wanted the main course, a whole fish, to be served with a lemon in its mouth. The maid thought this was a silly idea, and protested violently. Even threatened to quit. But Liz insisted. *Con un limon en la boca.*

'The maid agreed to serve the fish that way, thinking it was a stupid idea, but she relented. That night the ambassador and his wife were seated for dinner, and her face went pale when the maid brought out the whole fish on a silver tray, a lemon clenched in her teeth.'

Liz snapped. 'Stop, Jack. That's a stupid story. It was my fault. I didn't communicate what I wanted her to do. Why must you tell it?'

'Well, it's a funny story. You handled it well. You got him to see why it's important to speak the language.' Jack turned to his beef buyers. 'Here's another story. We had a maid we had to let go. She was an uneducated girl from the *campo*. We asked her to cook a chicken in the gas oven –'

'Jack, that's enough.'

'Can I finish the story?'

'I wish you wouldn't.' She looked at Jack with rebuking eyes and then at Jack's audience. She flared a smile. 'What he was going to say is that she filled the oven with paper and logs. She'd never seen a gas oven. We live in our own little worlds and don't understand how people can't be just like us. That's the story.' Her face had paled with awkward kindness toward the drinking men.

She stood. 'I'm exhausted, Jack. Do you mind terribly if I go home?' She turned to Katie. 'Will you come with me?'

'I promised to stay.'

'Then I'll go alone. I'll take a taxi. I'm sorry, Jack, I have a terrible headache. It's been a long day.'

Graham turned to Jack. 'If it's no trouble I can take her.' Mueller saw Liz briefly consider the offer, but whatever her hesitation it passed quickly, and she said, 'Kind of you, but that's not necessary.'

Lights dimmed as Liz made for the exit, and no one among the small group had the presence of mind to protest her departure. From the band onstage came beating drums and whooping calls. The band leader, in a rainbow-colored shirt and a headdress of threaded palms, shouted 'Diablo' to start the mambo, and the horn launched a catchy repeating rhythm that gathered in intensity. Dancers emerged doing a cha-cha-cha, slow beats done one, two, three, and there followed an up-tempo syncopated melody that drew a handsome couple onto the stage – he in tuxedo and she in a colorful flowing dress. Their precise footwork and acrobatic turns were the start of the show.

Mueller stepped back from the table and found a nearby pillar from which to watch. He observed the audience, and in particular watched Graham, now alone at the table. Mueller pondered him, pondered this man obviously trying to look at ease. Mueller slowly let his eyes drift back to the dancers – like a stage director watching the evening's performance.

A curtain opened. Props onstage evoked a plaza in Old Havana and into the spotlight of a street lamp strolled a woman in stiletto heels, carrying a sequined handbag, but otherwise naked. Her coffee skin, black hair, and scarlet lips were luminous in the bright light. She swung her handbag with a lazy arm and little acting skill, but no one in the audience was there to judge her acting. She used a come-hither finger to catch the attention of men prowling the plaza. She was joined by three other nudes in heels, elaborate feather hats, and rhinestone handbags, with the bored eagerness of women looking for business. The band played a rumbling percussive arrangement pierced by a bright whispery flute. The women came up to a passing car with exaggerated hip movements and whistles, but then the call and response to the driver was broken up by a policewoman who entered stage left.

She was a tall, voluptuous mulatto dressed in visored police cap and gold epaulets, and carrying a black truncheon – two feet long and rubber, that she slapped on her palm. She harassed the girls for soliciting customers and lined them up under the spotlight.

She had the first spread her legs and proceeded to search for concealed weapons. The harassed woman moved her hips rhythmically to the sound of a snare drum and the kitsch burlesque quieted the audience.

'Watch this.'

The voice was beside Mueller. Katie nodded at the stage. She had whispered her instruction when Mueller saw her, and she again looked at the stage. She added a moment later, 'They make more in a day than a cane cutter makes in a year. Young women wait hours for auditions. But it's a short career. The best get noticed. They go to Vegas or Miami, or find a man who supplies a visa.'

Mueller looked back at the garishly lit stage and watched one dancer be culled from the lineup. She was slight. He recognized Ofelia's raven hair and pearl skin. Her feigned surprise and mimed objections were grossly overplayed, but her youth and beauty forgave her amateur performance.

'She's Jack's girl,' Katie whispered.

Mueller watched the girl being put through a mock humiliation. *Jack's girl.* Mueller's understanding settled in, and with it the sense that it was something predictable, knowing Jack as he did, and that feeling deepened when Katie said Liz didn't know. Mueller felt the burden of the unwanted secret. He rehearsed how he would speak with his two married friends – graciously, thoughtfully, mindfully, but never again carelessly.

8

COLON CEMETERY

IT WAS LATER WHEN he retold the story that Mueller saw how absurd the whole misunderstanding was, and he found in the episode enough of his own fault that he used it as a calculated example of his naïveté, and in so doing he hoped to reinforce Jack's opinion that he was the amateur journalist. Everything he recalled for them was true but it was also true that he was glad to have the absurd incident to remove scrutiny from his assignment.

The incident occurred the morning after their visit to Sans Souci. At Jack's insistence Mueller had risen early to visit Colon Cemetery, taking the advice that any travel writer putting together a piece on Havana might want to highlight the necropolis. A spectacle of mausoleums. Great pompous structures with an air of grotesque comedy.

Mueller hoped to drag Katie along to take photographs, but she hadn't been in the lobby when the car Jack arranged arrived. So he went on the tour alone. Cemeteries had always fascinated him, and he'd been several times to Mozart's grave in Vienna's St. Marx Cemetery. These feeble efforts of the living to honor the incomprehensible. That thought drifted through his imagination, feeling as he did whenever he walked down the avenues of headstones, slightly displaced and awed, acutely aware of his place among the living.

His tour ended when he came to the wrought-iron gate where stonecutters displayed their inventory of markers for the cemetery's new inhabitants, and across the path, conveniently for bereaved mourners who would visit the new residents, sheds filled with elaborate wreaths and wax candles.

He heard his name called when he was gazing at the orchids, each delicate and aromatic. He looked up and faced a man on the other side of the gate.

'Señor Mueller?'

'Yes.'

'A car has been sent for you.'

'It was worth the trip,' Mueller said, stepping into the backseat, past the driver, who he noticed was not the same driver who had brought him out. 'My friend was right,' he said, 'a marvelous necropolis. As old as the ones in Europe. There was a funeral in progress.'

Mueller settled back into the seat and stretched his lanky frame. The day had gone gray and the tropical greens were lush, deep, saturated. He was glad he had come. Thinking tourists, the ones who needed a break from gambling and exotic floor shows, would be moved by a thirty-minute side trip to the city of the dead.

Mueller leaned forward and said to the driver, 'I need to stop by the hotel to collect my bags before you take me to see the others.' A moment later he saw the driver had turned from Avenida Carlos III toward the train station.

'Excuse me,' he said. 'This isn't the way to my hotel.'

Mueller got no answer, nor did the driver make eye contact in the rear view mirror. It was the man's determined silence and the odd feeling of being held prisoner that led Mueller to try the door. He found it locked.

'Who are you?' Mueller demanded. 'Where are you taking me?'

Kidnapped? Mueller considered the driver's position, his head vulnerable, the speed of the car. Mueller clenched his fingers, calculating the power of his fist, and then, while he was building his courage for a fight, the Oldsmobile pulled up to a gleaming marble portico surrounded by sandbags. The back door was opened from the outside and Mueller faced two men. One held the door and the other offered Mueller a hand. Both men were alike in their trim tan suits, narrow ties, and polished leather shoes, and both looked strong. Mueller saw no difference between them except that one had a thin moustache and the other was clean-shaven; otherwise they were similar and hard to distinguish. But then Mueller saw they were really not alike at all. The one with the moustache was short and smiled when he offered a helping hand, and the other was tall with a hatchet face.

'What's going on?' Mueller asked. 'Who is he?' Mueller pointed to the driver. 'This is a mistake. I didn't call a car.'

'Of course not, Mr Mueller,' the taller one said, bowing slightly at the waist, extending his hand. 'We are delighted to meet you. We sent the car so you wouldn't be inconvenienced.'

'What's this about?'

'Are you finding everything to your liking in Havana?'

'Not this.'

'Come with us. You're expected. It won't take long. The car will take you to your hotel. We have a few ideas for you as you think about how you'll describe our country. We are at your disposal. I have read your book.'

Mueller was startled to hear that, and the blandishment gave him pause, taking away his guard for a moment. He was led through a door, and passing a vestibule he found himself in a polished marble corridor empty except for a gauntlet of sculpted busts of dead Cuban dignitaries. At the end, the hallway opened onto a large office area crammed with secretaries typing. The din of clacking keys modulated as he passed desks and women looked up. Mueller navigated the obstacle course of manila folders stacked on the floor.

'In here, Mr Mueller.'

He found himself in a cavernous office with oil paintings, grotesque plaster molding, and huge casement windows shut to retain the cooling air from a wheezing air conditioner. A monstrous wood desk sat in the middle of the room, clear of all paper except one open file that held the attention of a slight man with gleaming black hair. Someone in authority, Mueller guessed by the way his two escorts held back when they presented him.

The man stood. Mueller detected the sweet, cloying smell of roses and he guessed it was the man's cologne. He was trim and compact and by some contrivance of posture and confidence he made the two taller escorts look short and cowering.

'Thank you for coming,' the man said in crisp English. His shirt was starched, his creased pants were wrinkled only in the knees from sitting, and he dabbed his lips with a monogramed handkerchief. He approached Mueller from across the room. He had piercing eyes and the air of a man conscious of how he was seen by others and careful to preserve his authority.

'I didn't have a choice,' Mueller said. 'I thought it was a mistake, but you have my name so it's not a mistake. And your man here claims to have read my book. So, I guess I should be flattered. But I want you to know this is quite ridiculous. Picked up on the street and brought here against my will. I have a mind to report it to the police.'

'We are the police. Let me introduce myself, Captain Alejandro Alonzo. Servicio de Inteligencia Militar. We won't keep you long. I know you are writing an article for *Holiday* magazine.'

Captain Alonzo lifted a recent issue from his desk and leafed through the pages as if it was a prop, before he returned it to the folder, and looked at Mueller.

'I have a few of your articles – the travel ones – and I liked your piece on Beirut. You found a way to express the city's complicated soul. Havana too is an enchanted city. Throughout history there are privileged moments when the genius of a people and lucky circumstances combine to turn cities into incomparable attractions – Athens, Alexandria, Venice. Few places are as exciting as Havana right now.'

'Boys hanging from lampposts,' Mueller said.

'We have incidents,' Alonzo said in exaggerated offense. Suddenly, he coughed from deep in his chest, a hacking cough. When it passed he dabbed his lips. 'Little incidents, but we have our famous cigars. We have casinos. We have your writer, Mr Hemingway. Tourists come here to sample what we offer – liquor, music, gambling, a taste of paradise. What more could a vacationer ask for? And now we also have our own little insurrection.' Alonzo said this without a trace of irony.

'I can be useful with interviews,' he added, again dabbing his lips. 'I suggest you speak with El Presidente and get his view. You will find him well informed and quoting him might give your article some authority. Don't you think?'

'Authority? Propaganda maybe.'

'We'd like a balanced picture of Cuba,' Captain Alonzo said. 'Here in Cuba we have a talent for making do with what is at hand. It gets us through our governments one dictator at a time.'

Mueller smiled. He gazed at the man and thought his eyes too large for his face. He exuded charm and reasonableness.

'I noticed you looked at the paintings when you came in,' Captain Alonzo said. His hand rose and directed Mueller to the fine art that decorated the pale blue plaster walls. 'This one,' he said, 'is by Marcelo Pogolotti, a painter who painted just fourteen years and then went blind. A tragedy. Then he became a writer and later a communist. This painting is called Palabra, done in 1938, and it's the work of a committed socialist. His politics were shallow and unfortunate, but his paintings are a fine expression of early Cuban modernism.'

Captain Alonzo shifted to the next canvas. 'This one is called Eva en el Bano. The tall nude was painted in 1943. Eva was the wife of a painter. She had an affair and left her marriage for a woman, scandalous at the time, particularly in a country tough with machismo. The insulted husband painted over the oil portrait to obliterate her. I found the piece and had the covering layers removed and the marvelous nude, thought lost, was revealed.

'Sometimes,' Captain Alonzo said, 'it's good to uncover the truth and sometimes it is dangerous to do so.' He turned and faced Mueller. 'It's a pity we don't have the truth about your friend, Mr Graham.' Alonzo's face hardened. 'Your photographer has also uncovered things that are dangerous. This morning we saw her taking photographs that reflect poorly on Cuba. The subject matter is disturbing. She bribed a corrupt policeman and now he has been relieved of his responsibilities, and you, Mr Mueller, have your own responsibility. She works for you. You must know she was taking photographs.'

Captain Alonzo's voice deepened. The charm and reasonableness Mueller had seen were gone, and in their place Mueller heard tempered disdain. 'There is a war on. We call it terrorism. They call it revolution. But it is a war. In war truth can be inconvenient.'

Captain Alonzo paused. 'As for you.' Alonzo handed Mueller a telex.

Mueller recognized it at once. It was his report to his editor with his first impressions of Havana.

'You can write what you like, but I am bothered that certain words appear too often in the text. The word "police," for example, doesn't have to be removed, but it doesn't have to appear eight times. Once is enough. Twice perhaps. I don't like the phrase "tremor of fear," which I don't understand. And there is an error in the report where you describe the last election as a corrupt event. I think you meant to write crowning event.'

9

ON THE ROAD TO CAMAGUEY

'WHAT I DIDN'T LIKE about him was his bogus charm.'

Mueller was beside Jack in the front of Jack's Land Rover, and he'd turned his head to the backseat to address Liz and Katie. The four of them were driving through a monotonous section of the Carretera Central several hours into their journey to Camaguey. Fields of sugar cane and thorn brush filled the view, and ahead, still a ways off, the russet hills of their destination.

'It was like a bad cologne,' Mueller said, looking at the two women, who had turned away from the window and gave him the courtesy of their attention. They smiled at Mueller's comment, but their eyes drifted back to the unchanging landscape.

'His comment to me,' Mueller added, 'when I said I'd go to the police and he said he was the police wasn't funny at the time. I was startled, but later I had to laugh. I suppose it should have been more obvious, but no one wore a uniform.'

Jack turned his head. 'They say he carries a wallet made from the tanned skin of tortured prisoners.' He looked at the tarred road. 'You've gotten attention at the wrong level, George. You're lit up. They probably know you're here in this car going to the ranch. Your press credential keeps you safe. But it has limits.'

Jack looked at Katie in the rear view mirror. 'What did you photograph?'

Katie continued to look out the window.

'What did they catch you photographing?'

Katie's eyes flashed indignantly. 'Someone has to be the interpreter of violence.'

'What did you see?' Liz asked.

'I'm not sure I want to say.'

'Why wouldn't you?'

'Fine. I got into a police station. They all have their own torture rooms. They have tile walls and drains in the floor so they can be hosed clean. There were bloody clothes on the floor and somewhere in the building a woman's scolding voice, and above that someone screaming.'

'Destroy the photos,' Jack said. 'It gives them an excuse to pick us up. Stick to packaged goods and bikinis.' Jack had raised his voice to be heard over the Land Rover's laboring engine. Windows were open for relief against the suffocating heat, but the whoosh of air meant he had to speak up to be heard, and that added to the impression of fractiousness.

Katie pretended to understand, and in a moment, had withdrawn her attention and gazed out the window again. Her hands grasped her camera.

'He say anything else?' Jack asked.

'About?'

'About anything.'

'He has an interest in Graham. Questions about Graham.'

'Don't we all,' Liz said.

It must have been noon. For some time they had been traveling on the improved, but rutted road, moving through ravines as it curved around hillocks, and then through untamed stands of thorn bush. Everywhere, to please the eye, were tall solitary palms.

'You're almost out of gas,' Mueller said.

'Half full,' Jack replied. 'It's your line of sight.'

'How far?' Mueller asked.

'Couple of hours.'

'Will we make it?'

'We'll make it. The thing has no power, which I don't like, but it travels great distances on a spit of gas.'

'Why didn't you fill it up at the last gas station?' Katie asked.

'Did you see the price? In Camaguey, I'd pay half.'

'He's thrifty,' Liz from the backseat.

'Frugal,' Jack corrected.

'Frugal,' Liz repeated.

'I can't hear you,' Jack said.

'I said you were frugal.'

He closed his window to reduce the noise. 'You're right. I'm frugal. I don't need to put money in the hands of thieves taking advantage of the fact they're the only gas for fifty miles.'

'Now it's hot,' Liz said. 'Open the window.'

'Turn on the air-conditioning,' Katie said.

'It doesn't come with air-conditioning,' Jack said. 'It's English. They endure the heat. Makes them feel superior to endure the heat.'

'You've never liked the English,' Liz said.

'What do you have against the English?' Katie asked. She turned to Mueller. 'Has he always had that view?'

'I don't hate the English,' Jack said.

Mueller turned and looked back at Katie. 'He spent an unpleasant winter there after the war, never comfortable with the English upper class.' He looked at Jack. 'Your loud opinions clashed with English reserve. You called it "a rainy weakened country with a big useless history."' Mueller laughed.

Jack looked at Mueller. 'Well, it wasn't original with me.' He spoke over the growling engine and cyclone of air. 'They lost their sense of entitlement after Suez. Shakespeare and the steam engine. What else have they done?'

Liz slumped in her seat. 'I'm tired of talking about England. Can we for once talk about something that you don't insult by tearing it down.'

'What do you want to talk about?' Jack asked.

Liz looked at Katie. 'What do we want to talk about?'

Jack had rolled up his window again, and Liz lowered hers a crack.

Mueller turned back to Liz and injected a question. 'Katie says you might be pregnant.'

'I didn't say I might be pregnant. I said I was. I miscarried.'

Mueller felt terrible, believing he'd steer the conversation to something positive, then hearing her confession.

'I'm fine,' Liz said. 'We've wanted a child for some time, so it was disappointing. There wasn't anything we could have done. We had good care.'

'We did not,' Jack said.

'I think I had good care.'

'You should have gone to bed rest.'

'That's my point. I didn't follow the doctor's advice. I should have.'

'Don't blame yourself. You always blame yourself. Next time we'll do better,' Jack said. 'You'll follow the doctor's orders.'

Liz had a brave smile. She looked out the window. 'Sometimes I think the child just didn't want to come out and be part of this world.'

'That's crazy,' Jack said.

'It's what I feel.'

Mueller saw a strange, sad expression on Liz's face that was a window onto a terrible grief. She gazed out at the barren, unchanging landscape of dry red earth on the passing hills. Mueller saw her lost in thought. He wanted to comfort her with a hand on her shoulder, but he was the friend, not the husband, and he was restrained by their tangled past. Her letter to him, in response to his note that he would be visiting Havana, had gushed enthusiasm.

A scorching sun was high in the sky when they turned off the main highway. Jack held the steering wheel firmly in his hand as he passed from asphalt to the gravel track, reducing speed. The Land Rover bumped along the narrow road that cut through impenetrable walls of thorn bush. They could see the road ahead, but the view behind was a clotted cloud of red dust thrown up by their tires.

They had been passing through this stretch of land for a while when Katie asked how long it would be before they arrived, and Liz threw out, 'An hour. Another hour of this.' She had closed her window to keep out the dust and the car had become stuffy.

'Liz, you're off by half,' Jack said. 'Two hours. This is the worst stretch. Not a good place to break down. Not even the squatters move in here.' Jack turned to Mueller. 'Have I told you the story about the squatters?'

'What story?'

'Jack!'

'Oh, come on, Liz. It's a funny story. I don't tear anyone down.'

Katie met Liz's eyes and mouthed, *Con un limon en la boca.*

Liz burst out laughing.

'What's so funny?' Jack demanded, sensing he was the object of ridicule. No one answered. 'Fine,' he said.

Jack turned to Mueller and continued his dissertation on cattle ranching, which had been interrupted. He said he'd brought Santa Gertrudis cattle to Cuba from Texas because they were better meat producers than the skinny Criollo and Brahman cattle native to the island. 'Cuba is perfect for cattle ranching,' he said. 'Rain, fertile soil, temperate weather all year round. Cattle like it. Yearlings fatten in the fall and we send them to Havana's slaughterhouses by train, then on to Miami by ship. My concern is the rail line. A month from now we transport the cattle and I don't want to find the rebels have shut down the railroad. We've put a ton of work into our place. Cleared out thorn brush, planted *colonião*. It's a guinea grass that is spongy with a lot of green leaf and almost no roots. It's easy on their hoofs. The only challenge we have – other than the occasional *precarista* who shoots at the house – is the tick population. The place is thick with ticks. We had to build dipping vats for the cattle.'

They drove on. The afternoon clouds had settled in and turned the sky the color of glue. Vultures in the middle of the road rose from roadkill when the Land Rover lumbered by. Thorn bush gave way to *algarrobo* trees as the road rose up the hills, tires on gravel spewing mushrooming dust. The land was parched at the higher level. The rutted, nameless road was marked only by peaked concrete stakes at kilometer intervals.

'Water,' Jack said, offering his leather *bota* to Mueller and the women.

Katie took a quick swig. She handed it back, admiring the embroidery, and then Jack quenched his thirst.

'Look at this land,' Katie said. 'Hot. Empty. Dry. I want a cool bath first thing when we arrive. I feel sticky.'

Then again the conversation turned to politics, as it always seemed to when other topics were exhausted. Low-grade anxiety of the unfolding uncertainty steered the conversation back to the topic. Mueller had not followed the conversation, but he listened when Jack dismissed Katie's opinion.

'Just because there is a filthy war on, I see no reason why you have to be miserable.' Then, sarcastically, 'You're young. You can afford the luxury of despair.'

Katie stared. 'I don't understand what that means. Would you explain what you mean?'

'I'm for the welfare of the people as much as the next man, but I have a ranch to run. Cattle don't feed themselves.'

'There is nothing worse than civil war,' Liz said,

'Defeat is worse,' Jack said.

'Worse? In what way? Worse than what we've got?'

'They're communists,' Jack said flatly.

'A dictator will be gone. We'll be free.'

'Maybe. Maybe we'll be free. But they'd take over our property. Nationalize business. We'll all be free. Free and poor.'

Mueller looked back at Liz, who glared at the back of her husband's head.

'Do you believe in good and evil?' Liz replied.

'What is good for one person,' Jack said calmly, 'may be evil for another, so it's misleading to talk about good and evil. We don't live in a monastery.' He nodded at the Camaguey plains. 'We live between the gangster colonels and the godless communists. Good? Evil? You tell me.'

Liz said, 'Yes, but people sometimes do good things because it is the right thing.'

'Why?' Jack snapped. 'Because they feel good about it? Is that the point? How you feel? You don't think Batista's thugs get a kick out of their work? I bet they do.'

'And there are people who stop themselves from doing evil because it *is* evil.'

Jack gave a look of strangled disgust that Mueller found almost amusing.

For some time they had been driving on the unimproved road, partly in a ravine as it wound around the hills common to that part of the country, and partly through untamed tangles of brush. Now they made a turn where the road curved around a dead tree and dipped to a bone dry river bed.

'What's that?' Liz asked.

She was the first to see the small group by the kilometer marker. Red dust kicked up from the road covered the stump occupied by an older man. He wore black and protected his head from the scorching sun with a white handkerchief he held over his head. It was meager cover. A young man in rags and sandals, a machete stuck in his belt, stood at his side. Beside them another skinny person. There was no shade where they stood. The road ran straight ahead to the riverbed, and on the other side climbed the next hill.

'What are they doing here?' Katie asked.

The sight of the three men had gotten the attention of everyone in the Land Rover, and the fatigue of the drive vanished. The group was just beyond the culvert, a spot where cars could safely pull over. They were poorly dressed, Mueller saw, their eyes looking at the approaching vehicle. The older man stood and lifted a water bottle that he pointed at, and to get across his need, he turned it upside down to show it was empty. His face was dark from the sun.

'What are they doing here?' Katie asked. 'Does anything ever pass by here?'

'It's a bus stop,' Jack said. 'The bus we saw a ways back, stopped. Broken down. That's the risk you run on this road. They'll be fine.'

'He's asking for water,' Liz said. 'Look, he's turned the water bottle upside down.'

They had gotten close enough to make out the old man's face, and to see that each of the men carried a machete in his waistband. Mueller saw only eyes, quiet, almost desperate, but straw hats obscured the faces of the other two men. Then he saw one was a girl.

Liz leaned forward. 'Jack, stop. They need help. They're thirsty.'

'They have machetes. I don't trust this. If we stop, we would not be safe if they attacked.'

Mueller looked at Jack and saw his friend's face, and saw there was no room in his expression to be inconvenienced by the travails of stranded strangers.

'We don't know who they are,' Jack said. 'You think you're being a good Samaritan and then when you've stopped they're on you.'

'They're thirsty Jack,' Liz said. 'She's a young girl. Jack, stop. For Christsake *stop*.'

'It's dangerous.'

'Dangerous,' Liz snapped. 'Where? Jack, they're alone. He's an old man. There's a girl. It's hot. They're thirsty.'

Jack steered the Land Rover to the left to avoid the group. Liz had her eyes on the old man, who came forward and held the water bottle up. Jack slowed down out of caution, but he held the steering wheel in a tense grip.

Liz reached forward and placed a comforting hand on her husband's shoulder, but he sloughed the attention and rejected her touch.

'Jack, what's wrong?'

Mueller felt the looming jeopardy and he saw in the dark corner of his mind where anxiety nests the danger they would be in if Jack was right, but he also saw only the old man pleading for water.

'What do you think, George?'

'Perhaps we should drive on.'

'I'll send a car back for them when we get to Camaguey.' Jack increased the speed of the Land Rover and he steered to avoid the man, who'd stepped into the road.

Liz was appalled. She looked at Mueller as if he'd betrayed her. She put her head to the open window and looked at the old man's wrinkled face, eyes pleading.

'You are heartless,' she said. She stared at Jack and Mueller, not comprehending their conspiracy against a simple act of charity.

'We will send a car back,' Jack said.

'He doesn't need a car. He needs water.'

'Close the window,' Jack said.

Bright sun and scorching heat turned the two men who had moved into the road into outsized objects. Jack steered straight ahead and maneuvered to avoid them.

'Jack. Stop now.'

'They have machetes.'

'What is it you don't understand about the word *now*?'

Liz took the leather *bota* that hung over the front seat and hurled it out the window.

Mueller felt the Land Rover come to a sudden stop. He saw a look of contempt on Jack's face and when he looked into the rear at Liz she stared back. Mueller saw in their faces the terrible truth of two people locked in a spiral of resentment. Mueller had no reconciling words to offer.

Jack put the Land Rover in reverse and drove back the short distance. Before stepping out of the Land Rover he pulled a Colt pistol from under his seat and pressed it into his belt.

He recovered the bota from the old man, who'd quenched his thirst and smiled in gratitude. Jack let him take another draught and he waited while the other two drank.

No one said anything when Jack slid back into the driver's seat. He tossed the bota into the back.

They drove on in silence.

PART II

1

CAMAGUEY

THERE WERE TWO CUBAS. The cruise ship Cuba of casinos and neon dance halls and the inland Cuba with its quiet, Spanish colonial past. Camaguey was the other forgotten Cuba.

'You need to write about this,' Liz said. 'There is this popular notion that Cuba is all about the Mafia, and that's true, but it's not the whole truth. You need to show the other side.'

It was the day after they'd arrived in Camaguey and Mueller stood in the portico of the Hotel Colon off the small plaza. Liz and Katie had arrived, as they had said they would, to start his tour of the town. Katie had her camera around her neck. A floppy hat and dark glasses protected her from the sun, and Liz was dressed alike. When Mueller came downstairs to the lobby, he'd seen them both and realized for the first time how alike they looked. They dressed alike, were the same height, had the same boyish frame, and if not for the Leica around Katie's neck he might have confused them.

They stepped into the midday sun. 'Camaguey,' Liz said, pointing out landmarks that made good photographs, 'calls itself a painted city. A painted city of red-tile roofs and pale walls colored from a broad palate of pink, rose, blue, indigo. The city,' she said, 'is a red dot on a dry landscape under a violent sun.' The cloudless sky radiated and throbbed carnelian blue.

Violent sun? To Mueller's question she replied that the city raised poets and she was reciting their phrases. Painted city. Violent sun. Radiating sky.

Mueller jotted down the phrases in his notebook. He wouldn't have understood the phrase 'violent sun' until he stood there experiencing the fierce midday heat, and the assault on his eyes of the blinding brightness. *It was indeed a violent sun*, he wrote.

Mueller followed Liz into the shade of the covered sidewalk that connected adjoining buildings on the plaza's north side.

'I want you to see *everything*,' she said.

It was the way she said the word that made him curious what she had in mind.

Fords and Chevys honked at a train of pack horses crossing the street, each horse under a load of wood, the neck of one tied to the tail of another. The cars waited as scrawny riders with sheathed machetes clattering against saddle leather kicked their reluctant horses with rusted iron spurs. There were indignant yells and aggressive honking when the lead horseman negotiated an intersection with an impatient taxi.

Mueller followed Liz and Katie through a warren of tight alleys and at each turn, as they moved deeper into the labyrinth of narrow streets, curious faces gazed at them from curtained windows. They passed through alleys twisting between stone walls, and Mueller expected at every turn that a door would open defiantly with the hostile face of a man with a machete.

Above, there were ornate black iron balconies and small boys who beckoned, and when you came close, they spat.

And everywhere they turned, rising above the low buildings, was the compass point of the cathedral's square tower with its fluted Moorish tiles.

Liz insisted they visit. The gong of the trolley excited her, and she pulled him along for the two-block ride, and then hopped off. She took his hand and pulled him along out of the sun through ponderous wood doors. They found themselves suddenly in profound darkness. As Mueller's eyes adjusted he saw the vast interior below a peaked ceiling, and below that, surrounding the upper reaches of the space, a skirt of dark stained glass depicting early Christian miracles. Dim light drew the eye upward. Blackened rafters crossed the ceiling. Profound quiet filled the rising space.

'This,' Liz said, 'was the last cathedral on the island to surrender its seclusion.'

Before the railroad, she said, there was only a dirt path connecting the city to the outside world. 'For two hundred years the city was lost. Jack and I fell in love with it.'

She pointed to the great gilt and bejeweled saints' images in the nave, which she said were carried through the streets on religious feast days, followed by crowds of children in white robes carrying candles.

On their way out they passed a Carmelite nun who slid by like a shadow, avoiding eye contact. It surprised Mueller and bothered him that he'd been unaware of her presence in the church. The nun wore a coarse cotton robe that covered her head to toe, and all he saw were her angular face and crusted feet.

Liz stopped at the door and looked back at the nave. Suddenly she took Mueller's hand, surprising him. He saw she was awed by the bloody crucified Christ.

'There is so much pain here,' she whispered. She turned to him. 'Come, I want to show you something.'

They had just been passing the end of the main square when Liz pointed out a nondescript two-story building among a row of similar buildings, but Mueller saw an armed guard at the door, which made it stand out. A small brass plaque read 'Cuerpo de Comunidad,' and below it were small porcelain facsimiles of Cuban and American flags.

'No one knows what goes on inside. I've had people tell me they've never seen anyone come or go. Other people have said the place is lit up late at night with a beehive of activity. Jeeps coming and going.'

Liz looked at Mueller. 'I'm told Toby Graham works here. Wouldn't that be a coincidence?'

There are no coincidences. 'I'll find out.'

*

Dusk darkened the stately home that sat on a low rise above the flat pastureland. Liz passed through the gate and drove to Hacienda Madrigal on a winding driveway. As they approached, the red ember sun bled through second-floor windows, making Mueller think the house was on fire. Liz's excited leap from the Land Rover dispelled the optical illusion. She insisted on giving him a tour of the house while Katie went off to her guestroom.

'You'll have to stay the night,' Liz said. 'Curfew is in half an hour and the roads aren't safe. I asked the maid to make up a room. Come, let me show you how we live.'

Mueller saw it was a colonial hacienda. A portico of arches and stone pillars wrapped the ground floor and at intervals there were clay pots to collect rain water. Lush plants hung from black iron rods that swung to catch the sun. A frieze of painted tiles scored the second floor's stucco walls, and windows on the balcony were thrown open for the breeze. Mueller saw how this sprawling home had once been a magnificent manor house, but it had fallen on hard times. Pink stucco walls were veined by water damage and wood window frames were bleached and cracked. He wanted to see the house as the pleasurable expression of his friends' adopted life on the island. Instead he saw only a gloomy place, a bleak place that held on to its decay against all efforts of restoration. His heart sank as dusk fell on Hacienda Madrigal like a curse.

Mueller followed Liz through the loggia with its pendant iron lamps until they reached two massive wood doors with muscular hinges that were thrown open. Once inside, he sensed the cooling smell of thick plaster walls.

She stood beside him in the foyer and pointed out blistering paint on cracked walls that were in worse shape than the exterior, but the obvious grandeur of the proportions hinted at vibrant memories of great wealth. Crumbling cornices, chipped terra-cotta floors, and faded plaster frescoes were work from the hands of master craftsmen employed as unrecognized artisans in a colonial time.

Everywhere he saw loving touches of repair, but all in an unfinished state, or abandoned. Old windows let in the dying sunlight and leaded glass depicted heroic mulattos cutting sugar cane. Furniture wobbled on the uneven tile floor and age bleached the blondness from wood, so it looked iron black. And then on one wall an enormous gold-framed oil painting of an unsmiling matriarch with her very young boy in jodhpurs holding a riding crop.

'Her husband built this place for her two hundred years ago as a wedding gift. He was Cuban and she was from Madrid. He built it to make her happy, but she was homesick. He tried to be a rancher, but he was never good at it. The house fell on hard times. Jack heard about it through a friend and when we visited we fell in love with the land, the house, everything.' She made a quick, energetic pirouette with her hand, drawing attention to the room as her body spun around.

'All the grazing land had gone wild,' she said, 'and the house, as you can see, was in disrepair. It's so *old*.' She smiled. 'Cuba has Spain in its past so I thought of all that charm, and only ninety miles from Florida. We can be there in an hour in Jack's plane.' She paused. 'We just had to leave Washington after all the hate and vilification McCarthy stirred up. Such a beastly demagogue, and a drunk, as it turns out. We thought we'd start a new life here. Come, let me show you.'

She took Mueller's arm and led him through an interior door and as they walked she clutched him and drew close, affectionately. 'I'm glad you've come. You can't replace old friends with new friends.' She continued walking and threw out, 'All this has been Jack's idea of what would make us happy.'

The door opened onto a large interior courtyard surrounded by the arched open hallways that ringed the private garden. Stone paths meandered through overgrown plantings of bougainvillea, hibiscus, orchids, and invasive weeds, all providing a rich fragrance to the evening air. One tall, spindly palm in the center was a lonely sentry above the hacienda. Bedroom doors thrown open for the evening breeze stood inside the hall that looked down on the courtyard. A swimming pool occupied the center of the courtyard. The blue water was illuminated from below by tiny lights embedded in azure tile walls.

'Jack's gift to me,' Liz said. 'He thought we'd spend the hot evenings here in the pool with our drinks.'

She quickly turned away from the swimming pool's brooding water and, darting past a bench cluttered with cast-off boots, straw hats, work gloves, all covered in a fine red dust, came to an open door. Mueller found himself at her side in a large formal room. Liz cheerfully pointed out the fine details in the layered tapestry of ruin. The wrought-iron chandelier was brought from Spain, she said, and a large beveled mirror had been made in Venice and transported overland by mules. Her hand swept across the room and she provided commentary on what the plan had been to restore the home to its former glory.

She stood in one spot before a wall bisected by an old faded pastel blue and a new rose wash. 'This is where we got to. We couldn't agree on the color. I wanted a cooler color to set off against the red tiles and he insisted we keep the original red. I said, "Fine, then do it." And it's been like this ever since. The wall divided by his red and my blue. I think this is where our marriage started to fray. Or maybe it had begun to fray before that, but this line seduced us.'

Mueller saw her soften her obvious hurt with a brave smile. 'I haven't told anyone this,' she said. 'There is no one from the old group who has come to visit. You're the first. I'm glad you came. Oh, we have friends here among the expats, and many are nice, but they're not old friends, like you, and this place is a small town in that way. I wouldn't feel comfortable sharing any of this.' She pulled him close.

Mueller wasn't prepared for her admission that the couple

he'd admired for stalwart companionship was coming apart.

'We bought the house *as is*,' Liz said flatly. 'And *as is* it has remained.'

She led Mueller through glazed French doors into a library. Double-height bookshelves lined the wall and upper rows were reached by a rolling ladder that followed a rail. Antique leather volumes were kept in glass cases whose door locks had tiny skeleton keys. Liz pulled one book from the cabinet and presented the worn cover and yellowing pages.

'Jack is a collector. This is Miro Argenter's *Chronicle of a War in Cuba*.' She added almost dismissively, 'The 1911 *Princips* edition. Jack's pride and joy.'

She shoved it back in place.

'Jack has a scout in Havana who finds these for him. He's an American with contacts in the Mafia who trades in antiquities. He bargains a good price from families liquidating their inheritance before fleeing the country, and he ships the books here, or Jack flies to pick them up. Jack doesn't believe Cubans will honor their legacy so he buys up the libraries. That is his excuse for hoarding.' Her hand swept the room.

'That's Jack. Snobbish at heart.'

'What does he do with them?' Mueller asked.

'Do? He collects them. He looks at them. He shows them to our guests. He is a collector. He has collected all this, the ranch, the library, this life.' Liz was suddenly quiet. 'That's not what I meant, but you know what I mean.'

She looked at the rows of bookshelves. 'He likes to say every library has a story. A beginning and an end. He says he is giving these books a new story.'

Liz looked fiercely at Mueller. 'I hate it here.'

They continued the tour, moving again to the courtyard

and then out to the grounds beyond the main house. She gave a perfunctory description of a tin-roofed barn that housed tractors, a pickup truck, baled hay, and a jumble of rusting machinery.

The sun was glowing red on the dark horizon when she took Mueller through the arched loggia. She suddenly turned to him.

'How do you know Toby?'

'Worked together.'

Mueller saw she wasn't satisfied. He considered what more to say, and what her interest was, and then he offered an anecdotal account of their personal history in college, where he'd known Graham and Jack, but they had not known each other. Mueller avoided any detail that compromised Graham, or hinted at his dossier. 'We were in the State Department together,' he said. 'Colleagues, acquaintances, friends. We've stayed in touch.'

Mueller spoke volumes but said little. It was his style to want to know why a question was asked before he answered it, and he didn't want to answer with information that had nothing to do with her question's intent. 'Why do you ask?'

'The group he works for – it's a front for something, isn't it?' She said it as if it were an accusation.

'I don't know.'

'Oh, George. You know. I hear it in your stupid vagueness. If you don't want to tell me, fine.' She stared at Mueller with a mixture of skepticism and disgust. 'This talk about an alternative to Batista has been going on for two years. Everyone wants a third force, but nothing has changed. Things have only gotten worse. You should tell your friends in Washington that they don't have a clue to life here.'

She cocked her head, eyes wide. 'They're caught up in their

gilded world. We have a country club ambassador and his clueless wife. That's why we left Washington.' Her face creased defiantly. 'I hate the hypocrisy and the lies. Maybe it's all we can expect in an imperfect world. But I wasn't raised that way.'

Mueller heard a minister's daughter's self-righteous tone in her voice.

'We were expected to go forth and do good in the world. We were told that from those to whom much is given much is expected. No one needed to explain this to us. It was all very repressed when I think about it. But we didn't complain. I just knew that I had to make the world a better place.'

Her eyes were alive and again she'd put her arm through his. 'Do me a big favor, George. Stay here a few days. Jack invited Toby to visit the weekend. I don't want the two of them to be alone together. I want company when he's here.'

It was warm out, but her hand was cold. Mueller felt her tremble.

2

CUERPO DE COMUNIDAD

MUELLER HAD INVITED HIMSELF to accompany Graham on a day's work with the excuse that it would give them time to catch up, and Mueller would get to see firsthand Graham's boast that he was making a difference among the rural poor and the squatters. Mueller believed Graham, but he knew it was a self-serving claim, and he wanted the authority of an eyewitness to amplify the exculpatory evidence he'd report to Headquarters. When Graham met him outside Hotel Colon, he mocked, 'Grab your pen. Give them what they want. Show them how I've changed.'

They drove out of Camaguey that Sunday morning in the soft light of dawn. Graham took the coast road and drove town to town in his jeep, from which all military markings had been painted over, Mueller beside him in the open vehicle. Graham moved easily among the *guajiros* with his colloquial Spanish, waving at puzzled faces that looked up from work as they drove by. Skinny, barefoot children rushed from houses when the jeep stopped in a hamlet. Everywhere pale stucco wash on buildings and children surrounding them with animated faces calling his first name, stressing vowels – Tobee, Tobee, Tobee. The children were bronzed, wild, and pleaded with open hands for his chocolate, or ball point pens, or cigarettes, which Graham disbursed to the mobbing kids. Then he opened boxes in the back of the jeep and distributed sacks of rice, cooking oil, flour – all purchased, he said, out of his own pocket because the embassy had no budget, or will, for community aid.

There was a sick child when they arrived in one hamlet, no more than a collection of houses that had sprung up roadside. Two men with urgent concern pointed to one house and spoke in guttural Spanish. Graham listened patiently, but his eyes drifted to a Cuban army transport and military jeep that were stopped by the salt flats beyond the hamlet. Ocean water fed shallow ponds and salt was harvested when the water evaporated. These were the salt farmers.

'Sí, sí,' Graham assured the pleading men, but he directed Mueller to the heavily armed Cuban soldiers who had fanned out on the narrow causeways between the ponds. Green helmets, tan fatigues, Thompson submachine guns, and each with the shoulder patch of a snarling lion.

'Who are they?'

'Policía Militar,' Graham said. 'Ribero's men. Thugs and butchers.'

Mueller stayed in the jeep while Graham grabbed his medicine kit and disappeared with the two men into the darkened house. There was no door, and cinder blocks of the first floor ended where rusting rebars sprouted waiting for the next phase of construction. An overcrowded bus spewing black exhaust sped by, sending rangy black hogs and children scampering out of harm's way, and when the road was empty again, they approached. An older boy with a tattered baseball cap and chipped tooth smile was eager to practice his English. He asked about the World Series and the Yankees' chances, then he asked for a cigarette, and as the conversation continued the shy younger ones closed in and gazed with wide eyes. Mueller asked what was wrong in the house.

'Hurt,' the older boy said. He smiled, proud of his English.

'Que cosa?'

The boy smacked his fist into his palm, then again, and threw himself to the ground. The younger children tittered nervously at the exaggerated pantomime.

'Choque,' the boy said, rising. He repeated his pantomime, slapping fist into palm, and his face calibrated serious concern. He pointed to the Cuban army transport and again smacked fist onto palm.

Mueller stepped from the jeep and entered the home. Closed shutters kept sunlight from the room and his eyes slowly adjusted to the space, dimness resolving to tolerable sight, and then he realized he was watched by a quiet group. No one spoke. The only sound came from a woman at the foot of a narrow bed who wheezed shallow breaths, something between pain and grief. Her hands were clasped prayerfully at her forehead and she leaned forward to the small child before her, covered to the waist in a thin sheet. Her face was puffed up, red, with swollen eyes, and she looked terrible in her anguish. She didn't notice Mueller, but an old man with a cane stared. Mueller saw three other adults – men and women – expressions flat, eyes calm.

Graham sat by the boy, his medicine bag open on his lap, and he was gathering up the instruments he'd removed. The boy had his eyes closed, hands at his side under the covering sheet. Mueller saw that the boy appeared to be sleeping soundly, deeply – removed from the concern of people surrounding him. He looked peaceful. His head was sunk into the pillow and his eyelids still and dreamy.

Graham stood. He whispered something to the grim father. The mother had not moved. She stared, grieving, at her dead son.

Mueller followed Graham out into the sunlight, and he heard Graham confide, 'They thought I could do something.' He lifted his bag of Band-Aids, antibacterial cream, gauze, and surgical scissors, shaking his head.

They sat in the jeep. Graham waved off the children who pushed forward. He looked at Mueller. 'It's enough to make you cry. Six years old. He ran into the road after a baseball. The pity is they thought I could do something for him.'

Graham turned the ignition. Unprovoked, he spoke again. He addressed Mueller, but he could have been speaking to himself. 'I've wasted time and now I don't want time to waste me.' He smiled at Mueller. 'It's taken me a long time to understand what it means.'

Mueller said the professor's name.

Graham smiled. 'Pompous teacher and a pederast, but otherwise a decent fellow. Big fan of *The Great Gatsby*. He liked to think of himself in that class of sad young men. Nothing to live for. Nothing to die for. I wanted nothing to do with him.'

They drove off in a cloud of dust, but upon reaching a small bridge on the other side of the hamlet they came upon the Policía Militar. The array of rectangular salt ponds and connecting paths was perfectly free of undergrowth. A long, decaying shack on the edge of a pond was crowded with weeds, and its sheet-metal roof rusted. Bleached gray siding had been poor cover for three salt farmers who stood before the squad of soldiers, hands cuffed behind, shirts torn, eyes claiming the ground.

'I know him,' Graham said, nodding at Captain Ribero. 'Worked with him.' The sun was merciless and reflected on Graham's forehead. 'Just follow my lead. He means to be menacing and he is.'

Graham slid out of the jeep, Mueller following, and they crossed the short distance to the perfectly still prisoners surrounded by threatening soldiers. Captain Ribero stepped forward as the Americans approached.

Mueller thought him tall for a Cuban. He was light-skinned, with a narrow, aquiline nose and gaunt cheeks. He wore silver frame sunglasses under a broad-brimmed campaign hat whose crown was pinched symmetrically in quarters. His uniform matched his squad's brown boots with tan leggings, flared breeches, and white ammunition bandoliers across chests. But Captain Ribero carried a Colt .45 in a leather holster and on the opposite hip a sheathed Bowie knife. Dry dust of the coastal plain covered his boots and filled in the dark creases where perspiration had come through his shirt.

Mueller saw it all at once. Three prisoners stripped of shirts, one already bleeding where he'd been struck in the ear. Nine heavily armed Policía Militar. Men and women from the hamlet gathered at the edge of the salt pond bearing witness. A pregnant young woman wept inconsolably, while an older woman comforted. Worried faces of the hamlet watched from a short distance.

'*Comunistas*,' Captain Ribero said to Graham. He spat. They had stopped five feet apart. The only indication they knew each other was Captain Ribero's shorthand judgment and the wariness with which they approached each other. 'Hiding there.' He pointed to the shack. 'They ran.' His hand made an arc across the maze of narrow causeways that crossed the open salt flats.

A fourth prisoner was being dragged from the shack, where he'd remained hidden when the others ran. He was made to stand apart from the group, his unsuccessful effort to hide now a crime. One soldier knocked him to the ground with his rifle butt and another kicked him in the testicles.

The soldiers stood beside their three prisoners waiting to restrain if one made a move to help. But none did. They stood erect, eyes forward, composed, almost stoic before the agony of their companion. They looked off at nothing to avoid letting empathy corrupt their feelings. They expected the soldiers to inflict pain on them too and Mueller saw each summon the courage for the ordeal that awaited.

Captain Ribero held up a new M1 Garand rifle, which he displayed to Graham. 'We found this. They shot my soldier.'

Captain Ribero walked to the three prisoners and unsheathed his Bowie knife. He walked back and forth in front of the captive men, speaking quietly to each, telling them he wanted the truth about who fired the shot, and that he would not tolerate lies. He held the Bowie knife, flicking the twelve inch blade toward their faces, snapping his wrist in a cutting gesture. He went down the line repeating his question, stopping at each man, staring into each frightened face, but he got no answer, so he did it again, this time raising his voice. His frustration turned to anger. It all happened in a second. His arm shot forward. He grabbed a young man by the ear, pulling him from the line, yanked back his head, and slashed his throat with the blade.

Captain Ribero resumed walking back and forth, speaking softly to the two remaining prisoners, resuming his request to know the truth, while the rebel who'd lost to Ribero's whimsy writhed on the ground, hands clutching a neck that bled out life. The two prisoners began to tremble. Shrieks of horror came from the pregnant woman.

Mueller yelled, 'Tell him to stop.' But, stunned, he had yelled this at Captain Ribero. Mueller turned to Graham, but Graham had already stepped forward.

'That's his way of getting answers,' he snapped, body tensing as Captain Ribero cut another throat.

'God damn it,' Graham yelled in his two-acre voice. 'Cut that shit out.' He leaped forward toward Captain Ribero, fist clenched. He strode across the dry earth, his intolerance livid on his fuming face.

Captain Ribero quickly slit the third prisoner's throat to show that he was not to have his authority questioned. He waved his knife at the one surviving prisoner on the ground. 'I have my answer.' He wiped his blade on the survivor's shirt and slid the knife back into its sheath.

He walked up to Graham and presented the M1 Garand. 'Where do they get these?' he demanded. 'Donde? Digame.' He walked off. The Policía Militar gathered in their transport and drove off along the coast road.

Mueller and Graham stepped back from the weeping women and grim men who collected the dead. There was nothing they could do. Not even the brilliant sun could lighten the dark pall on that patch of bleeding earth.

The two Americans returned to their jeep. Graham took a moment to speak, and when he did, he was bitter. He explained that the stories of torture and murder by the Cuban army, while hard to believe, were, as they had just seen, not exaggerations. He had reported these incidents to the ambassador, but no one wanted to believe the stories. No one wanted to have their opinions compromised by the facts. He said that torture and wanton killing had corrupted Cuban army discipline and no army that slaughtered innocents would prevail.

'And he was stupid. Three dead men. No useful information on the rifle. A whole town turned sympathetic to the rebels.' Graham turned the ignition and angrily shifted the stick shift into first gear. 'Idiot.'

The rest of the day unfolded in the same way as the morning, moving from hamlet to hamlet – but there were no more executions to contend with, and no dead children. Their mood never recovered from what they'd witnessed. Mueller stayed in the jeep while Graham went about his job dispensing food supplies. The day ended in a still and exquisitely brilliant sunset. The Caribbean shone peacefully; the sky was a benign immensity of muted blue, and they drove along the coast road exhausted by the morning's drama. Graham voiced his views on poverty, civil rights, the dignity of the human soul, and the stillness of grace he'd seen on the dead boy's face – a child whose future was taken by chance. A boy who remained innocent in his youth – who would never know the terrible corruptions of life.

Mueller looked from the passing landscape at Graham, surprised by his musing. Nothing Mueller knew of Graham's past prepared him for the transformation he heard in his voice. When had he ever heard Graham talk of sorrow and tears? It bothered him that he couldn't see through the charade. He had watched Graham, the Pied Piper, followed by barefoot children, and he tried to assemble a picture of the man who'd done terrible things – horrible things – over the years. Vienna, Budapest, Guatemala City. Mueller remembered what the director had said, how a man can change. We miss the signs and then when we see them we don't know whether to promote the change or contain it.

The memory came out of nowhere. Mueller looked over at Graham behind the wheel, eyes forward, and he felt a deep empathy for the man. That made Mueller uncomfortable.

3

CONTRADICTIONS

MUELLER HEARD LIZ'S LOUD call to dinner, the repetitions separated by the chime of a struck cow bell. His clothes had become infused with red dust after a day driving in an open jeep, and he'd put on pants and a shirt borrowed from Jack, which fit poorly. The call was a summons to the feast Liz had prepared to belatedly celebrate his visit.

Mueller was at the writing table when he heard Liz's call. He looked at what he'd written, trying to hold a fleeting thought against the distracting chime. He'd been prompted to write the details he'd witnessed, trying to reconcile opposing impressions of Graham – the man carrying a holstered pistol when he drove his jeep, eyes alert and wary, like a hawk, and the other man, the Graham who dispensed food, succored a sick child, found outrage in sudden executions. Mueller recorded these impressions, but he made no judgment, took no position. And yet Mueller felt the tug of evidence pull him to commit more than facts to the page. His fingers gripped his pen, his mind working with a feverish clarity to coax the shy thought that would make sense of the contradictions.

And then the chime. He looked up. The thought vanished. He pushed aside the journal. Mueller had been skeptical of the director's estimate of the time he'd be in Cuba, and now Mueller had exceeded by half even his own pessimistic view. He saw no way to reach a quick conclusion. He looked to the open window. The flat tableland was dotted with tall palms, and the air drifting in carried hints of squatters' fires clearing land. Night's coolness brought with it the sounds of insects. A full moon rose low on the horizon and it bewitched the sky like a glowing dragon illuminating the savanna. Stars were blighted by the approaching weather.

'The hurricane is approaching,' he wrote. 'I don't know what that means to my time here.'

*

Mueller had been seated at the dinner table when he saw Jack lumber in, arriving late, he said, after working at the dipping vats where a prize bull had stubbornly refused to enter. Jack was in a foul mood that he promptly sedated with a double scotch. His boots thick with red dust, his shirt stained with perspiration, he sat slumped in his chair while the interrupted conversation revived, but everyone at the table was aware Jack stared at Katie. His sudden appearance and his sullen mood put off the group. If he had something on his mind, or a gripe, he kept it to himself.

Katie, Liz, Graham, and Mueller sat across from one another at the long table in the courtyard, while Jack was in his usual position at one end. The sky overhead had deepened and a flickering candle had burned down.

'You destroy the film?' Jack asked suddenly. He refilled his not yet empty glass.

'The camera is safe,' Katie said aggressively.

'I'm sure it is. But that's not what I asked. What's on the roll?' Katie was quiet, defiant.

'What other pictures are there?' Jack asked. 'Any of us? Any of Liz? These people are not sophisticated but they are clever. You won't know the mood of the man who pulls you over until he is cruel or arbitrary. There is no appeal.'

'We should get her to Havana,' Mueller said. 'Then to Miami.'

'When?'

'Soon,' Liz said.

'How soon? Not with the storm that's coming.'

'Why are you in such a foul mood, Jack?' Liz asked.

'I'm not in a foul mood. Those photographs are dangerous. I asked her to get rid of them. She's a guest in our house and she is putting us at risk. She can come and go from Cuba, but we have this ranch. We aren't about to leave.'

Katie took four film canisters from the equipment bag at her feet. She opened one and exposed the long black strip of negatives against the flickering candle. She did the same with the second, third, and fourth rolls, dropping the curled strips to the patio. She glared at Jack. Her voice was violently polite. 'That should buy me time, shouldn't it?' Katie looked at the stunned faces around the table. 'I'm not being weak or compliant,' she said. 'There are other things more important than photos of faces, beaches, or a blood-stained bathroom. But now there is none of that.' She smiled hostilely at Jack. 'You're safe. All this is safe.' Her hand swept the courtyard.

No one noticed what Mueller had noticed. The others were astonished by her dramatic performance, and Jack looked satisfied, and Mueller was the only one who saw that Katie had destroyed her unexposed rolls and not the ones with the incriminating images, which were in a different side pocket of her bag. Mueller clapped at her bravado maneuver, but said nothing.

The incident brought the evening to a premature end. Jack rose in a righteous huff and lurched forward to Mueller. 'George, can we talk?' He looked at Graham. 'Alone, if you don't mind. You've got a room on the second floor, I understand. Ask Maximo if there is anything you need.' He called the short caretaker, who came hobbling from the kitchen. '*Ayuda el señor, por favor.*'

Jack led Mueller by the arm to the courtyard's gate. 'He's a good caretaker. Funny man. Good humor can make a big man out of anyone.'

Mueller walked beside Jack on the gravel road that led past the outbuildings and moved along the pastures that surrounded Hacienda Madrigal. Mueller knew that Jack's brooding silence trapped thoughts that were waiting to spill out. When he did speak, they were already away from the house, and his words came quietly, his feelings modulated to a flat note that revealed nothing, so Mueller had to listen closely. But he detected in Jack's voice a tentative quality and a hint of something he thought he'd never heard – vulnerability? Or was it fear?

'A pair of catastrophes,' Jack said quietly, not so much declaring himself as musing.

Then his mood changed again. He pointed toward the east where the evening sky was darkened by a weather front. High cumulus clouds rose in a black mass and deepened the sky's gloom.

'Hurricane Ella crossed the Leeward Islands two days ago,' he said. 'It's headed toward us.' He added, 'Here in Cuba even the hurricanes have English names.'

He smiled and then was silent again. 'It started as a tropical depression and strengthened to a tropical storm six hours later. By the end of the week it was a hurricane and it will make landfall in two or three days.' He kicked the dirt. 'Flooding will be the biggest danger.' Jack swept his hand across the dark shapes of his herd and then said, 'A big hurricane, which is what they are predicting, will flood the river over there.' He shook his head. 'It will take people's minds off the war.' He nodded vaguely. 'The rebels have moved out of the mountains and they're coming west toward us.'

Jack was quiet for a long time, lost in thought, but they had the durable bond of youth, which held them together through long periods of separation, and it made them tolerant of each other. And with that came casual trust. Jack, with his intimate relationship to the land, had taken the lead and was a few steps ahead of Mueller. Jack stopped and stared placidly at the cattle's motionless shapes. He seemed to Mueller unusually meditative. They stood in silence looking toward the western sky, a beckoning intensity without a speck to tarnish the dark canvas, but to the east, the dark clouds were an ominous harbinger.

'A pair of catastrophes,' Jack repeated. He looked at Mueller. 'I don't mean the hurricane, although it will be brutal and there's work to prepare for it, and I don't mean the rebel who fired on the house yesterday with his squirrel gun.'

Jack swept his hand across his holdings. The worst that could be said of him, Mueller thought, was that he'd grown up with an idea of himself that was out of step. He wanted land, but inside that sedentary man there was the spirit of the wanderer who was never satisfied to be in one place, or stay at home.

'I'm in a fix, George.'

Mueller was at his side now.

'That girl came to the ranch today. The foreman turned the taxi away. He told me about it when I came back from town.'

Mueller's confusion provoked Jack's response.

'The girl you met. The dancer. She came here today. Demanded to see me and made a big scene. Thank God Liz wasn't around.'

He kicked the dirt. 'She seems to think I promised her a new life, a Shangri-La in Miami.'

The gruff dismissive tone of his voice gave his comment an angry edge.

'She has these ideas in her head.' Jack's voice trailed off and he gazed into the night. 'Did I lead her on? I don't know. I might not have objected, so who knows what her mind concocted. That girl has been a bit of trouble.' He looked directly at Mueller. 'I have no intention of hurting my marriage.'

Mueller gave a choked laugh. Mueller pitied Jack's confident ignorance. It had always been that way in their relationship – Mueller the one who stepped in to help save Jack from the mess he'd made. Paid bail after he was arrested for drunken driving senior year. Arranged for a doctor in Harlem after Jack got a girl pregnant. It was George who rescued Jack from his self-inflicted wounds.

'I need a favor.'

George heard the request and in a way, he expected it. In an old friendship, the patterns don't change, only the stakes are raised.

Mueller looked at Jack and thought him pathetic. Jack had always been that way. It was locked in his character. Liz had seen it too, Mueller knew, and yet she'd been drawn to him. The Protestant minister's daughter in her had seen a case to reform, and she thought she could change him. Mueller had admired that about her. She thought she could make things right – a do-gooder, Jack called her, but he didn't intend it as a compliment. That was who she was. She'd found in Jack in the months before they married a young man confused about life, angry, lonely in the way you are when you get out of college staring with diminished ego at the hostile landscape of an adult world – and she'd taken him on as her project. And somewhere along the way in their marriage Mueller had seen Liz begin to weaken, to give up, defeated by the depressing cycles of anger and forgiveness that accompanied Jack's recidivism. And Jack, so full of himself, didn't see the change in his wife.

'Liz doesn't know about her, George.'

Mueller stopped himself from saying all that he thought. 'You're a coward, Jack.'

Jack raised an eyebrow. 'Yes, I suppose I am.'

Mueller stopped and stared.

'Will you visit the girl?'

Mueller was suddenly aware that Jack had not used her name, hadn't dignified her with a name, so she was denied the human face that came with a name, and she was just some mess he needed to clean up – and not a human being with needs, regrets, feelings, attachments. Mueller said the name: 'Ofelia.'

'Yes, that's her. Will you do this for me, George? Will you explain things to her?'

'Explain what? That you're a bastard?'

'Explain that I will get her to Miami. But she can't come

running over here. I'll get her out without a visa. No one is getting visas now. I'll fly her out. There's a private airstrip outside of Miami.'

Mueller saw Jack struggle the way he'd once done on the football field when he scrambled to recover from a disrupted play, ball in hand, thinking whether to pass or to run. He pondered his way out of a tight spot.

'She thinks I'll leave her behind. She wants to get away. She can't be happy here, married off. She has her dreams too, you know.'

Mueller thought that was the most empathetic thing he'd ever heard Jack say.

'I'll give you the address. She's in Camaguey.'

Mueller shook his head. 'The town is a warren of alleys.'

'Have Toby drive you. He knows the place. You can take the Land Rover. Calm her down. Tell her I'll fly her out after the hurricane. Will you do that for me, George?'

Mueller felt his contempt rise. 'Yes, I'll do it, but I won't be doing it for you.'

4

VIGIL

Toby graham was alone in the parked Land Rover looking at a closed carriage door just beyond a small circle of street light. He glanced at his watch and then without thinking he did it again. George, what is taking so long?

The attached house of two stories stood at the blind end of an alley with little to separate it from its neighbors. The space of sky above was a deepening blue and toward it the electric street lamp lifted its feeble lantern. The wooden door through which Mueller had passed did not give a hint that it would open again, and the balcony window remained shuttered. Other houses on the street, conscious of decent lives within, were quiet and impenetrable.

Again, his watch. He was drawn to another memory of waiting for Mueller that bitter cold January night in the Graben near the statue to plague victims. Soviet patrols kept Graham away from the warmth of a nearby bar and his fingers had gone numb in the alley. The wait then, the wait now. Old grudges rose up. Stubborn slights from the past came to mind. Graham had waited an hour in the freezing night and then Mueller hopped off the tram with his 'blind date,' oblivious to the scoped rifle aimed at his back. Graham should have let Mueller be the victim of his carelessness with the pretty double agent. The old grudges made Graham's skin itch.

A door slammed shut in the night. Graham sat bolt upright and watched a fretting Mueller approach the Land Rover across the stretch of dimly lighted street. Graham was in an uncharitable mood. He didn't have patience to put up with a man who had no sense of time, missed the danger signs, and was too eagerly an errand boy for a socialite friend.

*

'What took so long?' Graham snapped, turning the ignition when Mueller was seated.

Mueller pulled his door shut and looked into Graham's face. 'You were gone an hour. You said it would take fifteen minutes.' Graham tapped his wristwatch. 'Curfew starts in fifteen minutes. We'll be lucky to get back to the ranch without being pulled over. Arrested.'

Mueller raised an eyebrow at Graham's concern. 'I would have left if I could. I had no choice.'

Graham drove. He found his way through the warren of narrow, unmarked streets in the old city, but he had to double back when he discovered he'd made a wrong turn. The brace of delays had them come hard against the hour – and their risk settled in like a fever. Twilight. Too light for headlights to make a difference, too dark to make out the rutted potholes on the

131

road. Graham could only drive so fast before the Land Rover rattled violently.

'So,' Graham said, pausing, giving thought to what he might say. 'Pleased with the meeting?'

Pleased? Perhaps it was the silence that had settled in between them, or the abruptness of Graham's tone, as if he hadn't given up his irritation, or perhaps Mueller saw no reason to begrudge Graham the details.

'That's not the word I'd use,' he said. 'I was outside the door knocking. I'm sure you saw me. What you didn't see – and probably couldn't guess – I knew I was being watched from inside, so I tried not to be impatient. I'm sure whoever was inside wondered who I was and why I was there at that hour.'

Mueller found himself giving an account. 'Up close they were old doors with a rivet-studded surface to withstand forced entry, and heavy brass hinges. Understand?'

Graham looked at Mueller, confused.

'I want you to understand what I saw so you'll appreciate what happened. The doors were designed to keep you out – not let you in.' Mueller paused.

'After what seemed like a long time I heard footsteps inside shuffling on the stone floor. My visit had obviously gotten the household worked up. The door opened a crack. An old woman in black scarf over a wild nest of hair looked at me. Her face was wrinkled from the sun, but she had clear blue eyes that looked at me suspiciously. A shawl covered her shoulders. Light was dim and cool air flowed past her. She invited me in using my name.'

Mueller paused. 'That was the first surprise.'

He continued. 'I found myself in a large courtyard. Dogs growled at me as I entered, but the woman shooed them away.

High stone walls surrounded the courtyard. A team of horses and a carriage stood on the far side by a giant red clay pot that collected rainwater from the roof. A few straggling vines climbed the walls and a wild garden sat at the base. So, you get the picture. Outside, the home looked plain and weathered and ordinary, but inside I found another world. A private world. We have this phrase – a man's home is his castle – but for us the metaphor is all that is left. But there, inside that courtyard, and in the house, it was a castle – not in height or in grandeur, but you knew – I knew – when I stepped through those riveted doors I was inside a closed world. Keep that in mind because it helped me understand the conversation that followed.' Mueller looked at Graham. 'Are you listening?'

'I'm driving and I'm listening.'

'You should listen.'

Graham looked directly at Mueller. 'I'm listening.'

'I was led into a living room off the courtyard and asked to sit on a sofa. It had clawed feet, a velvet cover that was worn thin, and it looked like it had come from Spain a hundred years ago. I got the impression no one used the room except when guests were entertained. It had an empty formality, everything was worn or antique. Gold-framed portraits of dead relatives on one wall. You know how the eye picks up all these details and begins to form a story, so that's what I did. Old Spanish colonial family once wealthy now living under the yoke of poverty. There was a large crucifix with a tortured Jesus on the wall and below it tall wick candles and a leather Bible.

'I sat alone for fifteen minutes, maybe longer. I knew I was being made to wait and I assumed you were getting impatient, but I had no choice. Then, I was joined by a young man who entered from a side door. He sat opposite me in a large chair.

A determined face. Hostile eyes. He had black hair combed straight back. I was certain I'd seen him before, but I couldn't place him.

'"You want to speak with my sister," he said. He was polite, but his tone was challenging, as if to be there in his home was to violate the family. I replied that, yes, I had come to speak with Ofelia.'

'Does she know you?'

'"We've met," I said. He looked at me with thinly veiled disdain. His expression hardened and he rose suddenly. It was that motion, that sudden standing, like a jack-in-the-box popping up, that triggered my memory. I knew he was the man in El Floridita who'd shot out of his chair and shouted "A*bajo el tirano.*"'

'I recognized him, but he didn't seem to recognize me, even though we sat opposite each other in the police wagon – or if he did recognize me he didn't let on – and anyway none of that had to do with my visit. But then, I thought, of course he knew who I was and that's why the old woman knew my name. I said I'd be happy to speak with him if that's what he required.

'I introduced myself and he did the same. His name is Betancourt. He went on with a little lecture on Cuban manners. He said that Camaguey was not Havana and the bad manners tolerated in the capital had no place in his home. I told him I was there at Jack's request. I was surprised he didn't know Jack's name, but he knew the ranch.' Mueller paused. 'Look, part of me didn't want to be there at all, but Jack insisted I go, so I said more than I should have. But I don't think I had a choice. I was in the man's home asking to speak with his sister.

'He slumped in his chair and stared at me miserably, eyes severe and piercing. I kept thinking this man was part of the group that set off ten bombs across Havana. I leaned forward and explained that Jack was offering to fly Ofelia to Miami.'

"'My sister has no interest in Miami," he said. He waved his hand contemptuously. "She is a foolish girl with romantic ideas. There is nothing for her in Miami. This is her home. She has locked herself in her room."'

Mueller paused. 'Then I got the second surprise. He knew you were waiting outside in the Land Rover. He called you the Americano.' Mueller's long silence was a sign that he had finally come to the point of his story, and he stared at Graham with tolerant impatience. 'He said he'd invited me into the house out of respect for you.' He waited for Graham to comment, or share his opinion, but when no opinion came and no comment was offered, Mueller snapped, 'Well?'

'A lot of people know me.'

'Rebels?'

Graham laughed with jaunty self-confidence. 'Don't let your imagination take you to a place where we'll have to lie to each other.'

*

Mueller had been watching Graham navigate the pitted road with its potholes illuminated by the tunneling headlights. Mueller had taken Graham's cue and stopped asking how Betancourt knew of Graham, but he continued to speculate how the threads connected. At one point, he tired of the silence between them. 'I'm not Jack's doormat here,' Mueller said.

'He seems to need help.'

'His troubles have always been self-inflicted.'

'You'd do the same for me. That's who you are, George.

You've always helped friends when they got into a jam.'

Mueller heard the words and thought them unconvincing. The car was bouncing along and sputtering and it continued to do so before Mueller felt it regain a rhythm. 'How long have you known her?' Mueller saw that he'd confused Graham. 'Liz. How long have you known her?'

'A little while.'

Mueller restrained his impulse to ask all that he wanted to know – where they'd met, when, and how. He felt protective of Liz. He knew Graham's charm and he understood how women found him attractive, but Liz was not a woman who fell for those qualities. Liz, he suspected, didn't know who Graham worked for, or what he did. She couldn't know the dark stain on his life.

'Don't hurt her,' Mueller said. 'Do you understand? She is in a weakened state. Don't take advantage.' Mueller was calm, even friendly, but his words were threatening.

Their eyes met.

Graham looked back at the road, his face lit garishly in the dashboard's dim glow. 'She's miserable. You can see that.'

'Jack has always been this way. Liz knew what she was getting into when they married. She might have ignored it then, not wanting to acknowledge what she knew about him. But I don't think that was it. I think she thought she could change him.'

The sputtering returned.

'What's that?'

Suddenly, the Land Rover gasped, lurched, and came to a slow rolling stop. Graham turned the ignition, and with each twist he heard the battery weaken.

'We're out.'

'Of gas?'

Graham hit the steering wheel with his palm.

'I thought Jack filled it. He said he was going to fill it.'

'Is there a can in the back?'

Mueller didn't bother to look. 'We emptied it on our way out from Havana.'

'We can't stay here,' Graham said. 'We're an obvious target. We don't want to be sitting in this thing if someone decides to fire a rocket.'

They got out of the Land Rover. The night had become profoundly dark under a sky obscured by the advancing storm. Night sounds filled the dark world. They stood side by side and Graham looked up from the radium glow of his wristwatch. 'We can't make it walking. It's past curfew.'

'What do you propose? Too far to walk? Too dangerous to stay. You have a suggestion?'

'Words, words, words, George. Your mind has gone to mush with all that Shakespeare. Words will make a ghost of you.'

Mueller wanted to punch Graham. This was the confident, mocking Graham he remembered. Clever, petulant, obtuse, foul-mouthed, and within the space of a moment able to be dazzlingly considerate and insulting. Graham had never made a secret of his contempt for colleagues who didn't submit themselves to his mastery of a risky situation. Tongue lashings came easily to Toby Graham and it was the violence he'd survived that left him intolerant of others' errors. Mueller knew all that, and he knew too that Graham reserved his greatest scorn for the second-guessers in the Headquarters' bureaucracy, which he considered inept, bloated, incapable of making hard choices – men who saw each decision through the gauzy lens of selfish ambition.

'This way,' Graham said. Far off there was the faint glow

of a brush fire – land being cleared. 'There,' he said pointing down the road that disappeared into darkness. 'The next checkpoint.'

Mueller saw it too. A single dot of light strung over the road that dimly illuminated a low concrete guardhouse. The squat roadside building was small and vulnerable, surrounded as it was by a vast darkness. Second-floor light bled from one window, and but for that light the checkpoint looked abandoned.

Suddenly, far off, the crackle of rifle fire. The sound had no provenance in the dark, and Mueller was alert, moving his head a degree or two, but the sound could be coming from any direction. A mortar shell crumped far to their left. The flash of brilliant light bruised the night and a concussive blast followed. They stood absolutely still waiting for the next explosion, but there was only a long silence.

'Someone's taking an easy shot at a sleeping garrison. This won't be the offensive. The hurricane is coming. But one thing, George, you and I both know we don't want to be caught in the open on the road. In the dark, both sides will see us as the enemy.'

Thudding mortar fire came a second time far off and it was mixed with short bursts of rifle fire.

'Rebel mortars,' Graham said. 'Soldiers returning fire. Listen. Long bursts, shooting into the dark. Fear firing. Rebels don't have the ammunition to waste like that. Let's go. No need to run.'

They approached the pool of light that illuminated the checkpoint. Graham restrained Mueller's arm when they came to the light's perimeter. 'We don't want them to think we're sneaking up on them. They are more frightened than we are.'

'What's the plan?'

'We ask to spend the night. It's too far to walk to the ranch.'

'I could make it.'

A guard emerged from the door at the top of the outside stairs and waved them forward.

'Now we don't have a choice.'

Graham called out a greeting in his fluent Spanish, and Mueller understood most of the conversation that followed, including Graham's explanation that they'd run out of gas. The two Americans stood before the steel counterweighted stanchion that lay across the road, and Mueller felt himself the target of the soldier's raised weapon.

'Okay,' Graham said. 'They'll let us stay until morning.'

Mueller felt Graham's hand on his waist. 'Don't let them see that.'

Mueller had taken the Colt pistol Jack kept in the Land Rover, but now he stuffed it under his shirt. Mueller followed Graham up the concrete steps to the waiting sergeant, who'd lowered his bolt-action Springfield rifle, stock gripped in one hand, barrel angled to the floor. Mueller knew the outposts were manned by a second class of soldier pressed into service with little training, given uniforms harvested from dead comrades. He saw this in the young soldier's eyes, dark, anxious, uncertain, pretending authority over his ten square meters of command. Mueller understood enough Spanish to recognize Graham's exaggerations. It didn't matter. The sergeant didn't need the actual story, just a credible account that made it feel safe for him to host two strangers.

Light Mueller had seen through the slatted window came from a propane burner's flickering flame. Two soldiers, teenagers, Mueller guessed, sat on haunches and stirred a pot of black beans. A fourth soldier sat on the concrete floor, back against the wall, legs splayed. The room was bare except for rifles, a few rolled blankets, the sputtering burner, and a hint of urine.

Eight hours to dawn. 'We're better off walking,' Mueller said. 'And risk getting shot?'

The soldiers were young, skinny, in ill-fitting uniforms with the dulled affect of men accustomed to endless waiting. The sergeant's shoulder patch was one sign of rank, his black boots the other. His men wore sandals. Machetes and two Springfield rifles stood by the door.

Graham slid against the wall with the bowl of beans he'd been offered, and fed himself with his fingers. Mueller passed on the meal.

'See the guns?' Graham said. 'Appeal to your sense of irony? The embargo has turned Batista's army into a pathetic fighting force. You see the result. Army in name only. All the weapons go to SIM and Policía Militar. You know the result.' Graham nodded at the scar on Mueller's forehead.

They sat quietly, each looking at the boy soldiers eating, eyes watching suspiciously, and Mueller again looked around the room, but there was nothing he had missed in his first survey, and the only change was in the soldiers' faces, done feeding themselves with cupped fingers.

Graham offered to share his bowl with Mueller. 'It might be your last meal.'

'I'll take my chances.' This was the Graham Mueller remembered. The joking choice of mortal outcomes carelessly thrown out like a dare. This was the man he'd known, whom he'd come to grudgingly respect even when he didn't like him.

Mueller gazed at him at home on the floor, using his fingers to eat. He reflected upon this son of the American South, a redneck born in the Mississippi delta whose salesman father was a part-time con artist who moved the family to a farm in Ohio to build a better life, and then abandoned his wife and son. Graham's neck tanned whenever he spent an hour in the sun, and Mueller had seen it happen on summer days in Austria organizing farmers, when his ruddy neck and arms simply got redder.

Mueller thought him a runty man when they first met, Mueller's lanky frame rising a head above Graham, but it was Graham who commanded. His unusual physical stamina and equally unusual assertiveness made up for his lack of stature. He had always been the one who worked long hours – longer than most – putting in twelve-hour days and surviving on five hours of sleep in the field.

His assertiveness didn't show in his soft tenor voice, but if he got excited, and Mueller had seen him very excited at times, particularly when he saw laziness in others, Graham had a brisk way of letting you know he was displeased. He always seemed to Mueller the kind of man who knew what he wanted to do, and how he wanted to go about doing it.

Details fascinated Graham. He prized facts. He absorbed great quantities of them and when he needed more to complete a picture, he searched relentlessly until confident he had all the facts needed to solve a problem or make a judgment. He was of a class of deeply optimistic men, Mueller knew, and he knew this because he recognized himself in Graham, who had lived through World War II, who believed in the power of an idea – who believed that any challenge could be overcome by will power, and by money, intellect, and when necessary, covert action.

Hungary, Austria, Guatemala. He'd been on the bayonet

borders of the Cold War. He'd driven mountain roads in Guatemala that no one else would drive just to prove they could be driven, and in the process, he'd been shot at twice, wounded once. Stories collected around Graham. He took risks that frightened other men. The odds, he boasted, didn't apply to him.

Mueller was not jealous of Graham, or only occasionally so, when he stood at the mirror, a little resentful of life, unhappy he'd grown older without any proud successes, perhaps his own fault, to be sure, but luck too had been against him. In those moments, Toby Graham came to mind as the schoolmate who'd come close to fulfilling his early promise. He'd kept at it and hadn't let disappointments sap his resolve. Mueller admired Graham for staying in the game – chalking up enough promotions to keep admirers whispering. If Mueller had felt better about himself, he wouldn't have given in to envy. But he resented Graham because he was naturally good at his job – good at most things – good with women who found him attractive because he wasn't caught up in boasts, or weighed down with sorrows, and he seemed indifferent to fame and failure. And yes, Mueller resented the poor farm boy Graham who made good and made success seem easy. Mueller smiled at Graham's predicament, but he didn't take satisfaction in his misfortune. He'd stayed in the game and tried to make a difference, and Mueller admired him for that. There it was. Ripe jealousy and its twin – reluctant admiration.

*

'You can't imagine what this war has become, George.'

Mueller had closed his eyes. He found Graham fully awake,

alive in the silence of the room, his mind restlessly engaged by the quiet. The old spirit fatigued.

'American reporters want a good story – and some of them want to believe Castro is a hero. They've invented him, you know, the *Times* did, when Matthews found him alive in the Sierra Maestra miraculously resurrected. And now it's hard to book a hotel in Havana. Newsmen are flying in to witness Batista's fall. Everyone wants to be there when the end comes.'

Graham looked at Mueller. 'I'm surprised they sent you down as a travel writer. It shows how out of touch they are, thinking a journalist assigned to cover casinos in a war zone is a credible cover. Christ, George, now you know what I'm up against.'

Mueller waited for Graham to add to his outburst, but he saw that he'd used up his rancor. This was the field officer's complaint. Headquarters never understood the dynamics on the ground. Desk men preferred the elegant, but utterly impractical operation that fit nicely into a memorandum. You were told to accomplish a goal and it was understood the methods used were whatever the situation required so long as the Agency's involvement, if discovered, could be plausibly denied.

Somehow they'd gotten on to another topic. Mueller heard a change in Graham's voice, a drop in register that sounded like the prelude to an admission.

'I was there, you know.'

Mueller looked at Graham, confused. *Had he missed something?* 'Where?'

'Guatemala City. The last days of PBSUCCESS. It was the same type of thing we ran in Vienna, rolling up communist networks and collaborators. We were to take out Árbenz and install Castillo Armas, which we did. It was done well, like a flawless production of *Richard II*.' Graham winked. 'A corrupt man infused with self and vain conceit.'

'I didn't know.' *A lie.*

'Four years ago. We ran a radio station that broadcast from a ship anchored two miles offshore. We used call letters of a Spanish-language station in Miami, so it sounded like a real radio station, and the radio announcer read news reports of a large invading army entering Guatemala from the north whose goal was to unseat Árbenz. The announcer reported that a B-26 bomber hit an oil refinery outside the capital, and an armor-led, air-force-backed army was invading. It scared the bejesus out of Árbenz.

'We had a good time writing the scripts for those broadcasts,' Graham said. 'We turned one rickety bomber and a pathetic squad of fifty-six poorly trained soldiers into a Roman legion. Well, it worked. Árbenz fled.'

Graham paused. 'We knew we didn't have a good shot at a coup. We had no resources and Árbenz had been democratically elected so there was no chance we'd foment a popular uprising. What's the saying? If you have the law, argue the law. If you've got the facts, argue the facts. If you have neither, raise your voice and pound your fists. Well, we had no army, no air force, no popular support, but we had a radio transmitter and a clever copywriter. We hired the press relations guy from United Fruit. He wrote the script. He was an old radio guy who remembered Orson Welles's *War of the Worlds*, and he came up with the idea. It was a bright shining lie.'

Graham laughed. 'They thought we could do the same here, but Castro works the press better than we do. Matthews's frontpage piece in the *Times* said Castro was alive and he had a wellarmed force. Remember that? Well, Castro marched the same six rebels around the mountain camp in different hats so Matthews became convinced there were a hundred well-armed men.'

Graham paused, eyes alert to sounds. Full-throated croaking frogs drifted in from outside. Soldiers had dozed off. Even the sentry on guard duty at the door had closed his eyes.

'I was lucky,' Graham said, voice deeper, quieter. Thoughts stirred by his account nested in his mind. 'Our radio victory meant we didn't have to create "K" groups. The killers.' Graham paused again. He looked at his clasped hands.

'Some things changed in the Agency after you left. I saw it in Berlin. There was coldness in the thinking. The planning. A sterility. Violent methods. New bureaucrats hired to fill desk jobs – and they played the game without ever having been in the field. Artichoke interrogations were done in teams of three. We used sodium amytal, sodium pentothal, and LSD, often together with beatings. Artichoke explored whether a man under drug influence and hypnosis could be made to assassinate a target. Interrogations used electric shock to produce convulsions and eventually, they hoped, amnesia, wiping out the memory of murder. I was there. I was in the room. Men died. It was all concocted by ambitious men thinking they were playing a Cold War board game. Do you know what I'm talking about? It was a feeling I got – hard to put into words – these perfectly decent Ivy Leaguers at their desks writing memos on extreme interrogation and assassination. We were given a manual on the best ways to extract a man's eyes to keep him alive, but blind, one eye at a time, to get a confession. Decent men, ambitious men, who were asked to rationalize assassinations so they wrote a manual on the most effective way to kill. I got the manual in Guatemala.

'The tone of the manual was appalling. Assassination is a terrible, horrible choice. A last resort. None of that came through. It laid out the best way to kill a popular and democratically elected head of state. This may seem like a small distinction, but the memo crystallized for me the changes I'd seen in the Agency. Too many men thoughtlessly representing the popular prejudices, the political rhetoric, doing what they thought would get them promoted, if you want to be cynical, and gone from the Agency were the good men – like you, George – good men with built-in, shockproof shit detectors. Where was respect for human decency?'

Mueller was surprised by Graham's righteous tone. He turned to look. He saw in Graham's eyes, in his clasped hands, heard in his voice, the struggle of a man suffering the moral hazards of his work. Mueller knew he was the closest thing Graham would have to a confidant.

So, Mueller thought. *These were the opinions the director wanted to uncover.* A man at war with himself. Good men were expected to question the work from time to time, and if they didn't they probably weren't fit for the job. It wasn't the doubt that interested Mueller. Doubt was a healthy tonic. But what had Graham done with his doubt?

*

It was past midnight when Mueller awoke. In his sleep, he had drifted in and out of consciousness, his mind still working, but dulled, asking itself what to make of Graham. Asking itself if he was asleep even as he slept, aware of sounds of soldiers shifting position, and the tremor in the concrete from a far-off mortar shell. His mind catalogued each sound without opening his eyes.

Mueller lifted his head off his knees and saw Graham was gone. Mueller found him just outside the open door gazing into the night. Distant tiny fires glowed where the canopy of darkness met the ambiguous horizon. A hint of smoke hung in the air. Mueller looked at Graham, quiet and still, like a sentry at a gate.

'Oh, it's you,' Graham said. 'Look at this.' He nodded up at the evening sky. 'You won't see those stars in New Haven.'

Mueller followed Graham's line of sight through the gathering clouds, but seeing nothing to keep his attention he looked at the surrounding brush. Mueller listened. It had to be late. He glanced at his watch and saw that dawn was hours away. They stood side by side, silent under the entombing sky.

'What were you looking for?' Mueller asked. 'When I came out I saw you looking at something.'

Graham shot a glance back into the room. One soldier was slumped against the wall, another gazed at them – big eyes, bare feet, hands clutching a rifle.

'I don't want us caught here if a mortar round is lobbed in.' Graham undid his pants and peed off the balcony. Graham spoke quietly over the sound of his urination. 'They don't have a clue.'

There was a beat of silence.

'Can I ask you a question, George?' Graham hitched up his pants. 'It's easy and useful to do what is expected of you however many doubts you might have, but you know in this business regrets accumulate and you get to that point in your life, at least I have, when actions don't align with consequences. I don't want to sound foolish, but you get to a point where it's hard to stomach the hypocrisy of it all, the self-serving commandments from Headquarters.' He looked at Mueller. 'Is that what you want to hear? That what they worry about? Why they sent you?'

Mueller said nothing.

Graham turned back to the ambiguous darkness and the sounds of bleating frogs and continued in a confessional tone. 'I could pretend it doesn't bother me. The ineptitude. State Department embargoing arms to feel good about themselves when they go to Sunday church service. Pryce poking around like a coroner, looking to embarrass us. And the work here – hedging our bets against the wrong outcome. I can dress myself up in lies as well as the next man; blind myself to the hypocrisy. Disloyal?'

Mueller looked at Graham.

'Disloyal?' Graham repeated. 'Perhaps. Disloyal to what? To lies and hypocrisy? I will die, as we all will, each of our lives bracketed by sleep. We all want to die well, to be relaxed about it, and hope to leave this world a good-looking corpse.' He added, 'I want my epitaph to read, "Here lies a good man."'

'It's too late for that,' Mueller snapped.

'Perhaps.' Graham took the Colt pistol from Mueller's belt. Darkness hid his movement from the room. 'I've unwound a coil of doubt that only this will succor.'

Mueller stiffened. He saw Graham point the gun at his chest. The two men were close enough to feel the warmth of their breath. He felt Graham place the cocked pistol against his heart.

Graham whispered, 'You know things that make you dangerous to me.'

The two men gazed at each other, one moment becoming two. Mueller went cold.

'I could shoot you, George.' Graham smiled. 'Violence is what I know. And I suppose I do have a gripe against you –

coming down here on the pretense of, what? Making me into a traitor?'

'Are you?'

'Traitor?' Graham coughed his laugh. 'Nothing good or bad but thinking makes it so, George. You know the line. You're the expert. Think of me as a mortal soul who knows only the vocabulary of violence, and has now found a way to put that talent to a good purpose.'

Mueller listened.

Graham leaned forward. 'Think, George. Think. Who is the enemy here? You were good at that. You were the one who told me it's never who you think it is. Remember Vienna? The gunshot. Our "blind date" with the KGB walk-in. Not who we thought she was.'

Graham slipped the Colt back into Mueller's belt. He smiled again. 'People don't like what I'm up to. Remember who I am.' He turned back from the sleeping soldiers. 'The challenge for me – for us when you were working for us – is the persistent contemplation of evil, and that's what we do, we start with the notion that we are in a battle with the forces of evil. The human problem is that it leads to pessimism and pessimism weakens the soul. I have seen the darkness – and I've felt its gravitational pull. I have trained death squads. Did I pull the trigger? No. But men died. I gave them the gun and showed them where to place the finger. It was my job.' Graham suddenly quieted. 'It happened to you, George.'

'I was never in as deep as you,' Mueller said.

'You got fed up and left. That's what I meant. You got out.'

'That's what this is about? Leaving the Agency?'

'That day comes for all of us. It's only a question whether it's a time of your choosing.' Then, almost dismissively, 'I am doing my job. I'll finish the work.' He paused again. 'Think about what they're really worried about.'

Mueller was surprised by the remark. It was just like Graham to plant a thought. 'About what?'

Graham didn't take the trouble to answer.

Mueller wanted to ask his question again, but he didn't. It wasn't worth asking. He'd get the same answer – or no answer. There was something he wasn't supposed to know. He knew he was in a labyrinth. There were no morals except in relation to each other. You lied to spouses, to girlfriends, to children, to parents, to Congress, but never to the director – and never to yourself. This was the trust built into the tight fraternity of colleagues whose lives depended on each other. The work required you to subvert popular leaders, bribe politicians, mislead senators, suborn friends – all within the moral gloss of a world in which ends justified the means. They did not judge each other by what they did or how, but by their accomplishments. Their fraternity was the secrets they kept. Mueller recognized Graham's warning.

The two men stood chatting for a long time. Half-finished thoughts came between them, occasionally broken with the sloppy wording of unrehearsed memories. Two men removed in time and place, far away from anything familiar, free under the sheltering sky to speak openly about everything but the one thing that had brought them together. Mueller knew Graham's record, knew how the self-schooled farm boy talked his way into college, but he also was certain he knew only a fraction of the man's 'successes.' Graham's redacted dossier he'd been shown by Lockwood cast a shadow over their conversation.

Mueller recalled Lockwood's comment. The incident with the woman in Guatemala. It was always a young woman, they said. Love and danger slept in the same bed. She'd been a pretty thing. A Guatemalan in her early twenties who'd become Graham's girlfriend, but she had paid a price for their acquaintance. Árbenz's thugs had raped her, slit her throat, and tossed her body by the side of the city's sewer. Graham had gone quiet for a few days and then reported the incident phlegmatically, almost without sentiment or remorse, as if a show of emotion would weaken him. That's what Lockwood had said, offering his opinion. Graham had steeled himself against whatever guilt he felt for putting her in harm's way. That's what they did, what they trained for, what was expected of them. Lockwood had said, 'Well, he's not a priest. None of us are. We're spies.'

Mueller looked at Graham leaning on the balcony, eyes gazing into the brooding darkness. Silence enveloped them in a mood that was not quite like grace. Mueller wondered. *So, what else has changed?*

Mueller got his answer a moment later. Graham released his clasped hands, then closed them again, clasping and unclasping, and a great heave filled his chest.

'Has she talked to you about me?'

'Who?'

'Liz. I'm talking about Liz. Has she asked about me?'

Mueller said she hadn't. Mueller volunteered how he knew Liz, some of which he'd shared before, and he was surprised how Graham took it in, as if he were hearing it for the first time. Mueller felt he could say anything about Liz – her hair color, shoe size, favorite food – and Graham would be fascinated.

They talked in the way one does late at night, prisoners of the hour. Reticence vanquished by elastic time. Mueller saw Graham look up from time to time when he heard far-off gunfire, alert for an instant, but then he returned to their conversation.

'You know what happened to me in Guatemala,' he said. 'I was hardened, single-minded and full of myself – caught up in the game and our cleverness. Aware too, I suppose, that I was becoming all about the boast.'

Graham reflected. Silence lingered. 'Then I met Liz.' He looked at Mueller. 'Yes, in Guatemala. I didn't want it to happen again. The Guatemalan woman had been dead a month. But Liz was a bright, lively person, a caring woman, who converted me with that smile of hers. And she saved my life.'

'Saved your life?'

'She can tell you the story if she is willing to be open about it. I knew I wanted her, but I had nothing to offer her except my grief and misery. And she was gone before I could express any of it. I woke the fifth morning and she was gone. I was ready – eager – to have her, and I could see she was looking for something. I could see that she was unhappy, but at the time I didn't know she was married. She was too conventional to give up a bad marriage for a man she'd just met. I suspect it was easier for her to have several days of fond memories than a lifetime of regret. We would have sunk into a quagmire because we weren't right for each other – then.

'I didn't follow her. She left a note, but no address. I sucked up the hurt, but I could not bury the memory. I thought: *I am destined to live my life with a heart that yearns for a moment I didn't seize.*'

Graham looked at Mueller. 'We grunt and sweat under moral duress in this job. Conscience weighs heavily but only for some of us does conscience offer a way out. I woke up one morning and thought that I'd live the rest of my life alone. Doing what?'

He looked at his companion. 'Betraying friends?'

Mueller saw that Graham had slumped on his elbows. Never did Graham expect to hear Graham confess so honestly.

'She didn't expect me to find her,' Graham said. 'I don't think she knew I was here until you brought up my name. Apparently, it came out while you were in the hotel. That's what she told me. It's an odd coincidence that you, George, of all people, connected us. It would have happened without you, but it was the excuse I needed to introduce myself to her again.'

Graham was suddenly alert. His body had gone rigid, and he cocked his head to one side, listening. His eyes were raptorlike.

'What is it?'

'Look with your ears.'

Mueller closed his eyes and listened.

'It's a *trogon*.'

A hollow, throaty bird below them sang *toco-toco-tocorotocoro*. Not far away a mate repeated the sounds twice, a call and response.

'Time for a walk,' Graham whispered. 'Follow me. When I go down wait a minute, then follow.'

'My hat?'

'Leave it,' Graham said briskly. 'We are going for a pee if they ask. I'll tell them that. Just keep moving.'

*

Mueller watched Graham siphon gasoline from the army jeep parked by the lowered stanchion. They got the fuel they needed, filling a plastic container they'd found at the base of the stairs. The two men had gone two hundred feet from the checkpoint when Mueller heard the *whoosh* in the cane field. A moment later the blockhouse exploded in a brilliant phosphorous white. The concussive blast hit them. Mueller found himself running away from the leaping flames that consumed the checkpoint, trying to stay up with a sprinting Graham.

Mueller worked his arms hard to keep close to Graham, shorter than Mueller, but with the advantages of being fit and a fast stride. Mueller tasted sweat that formed on his upper lip. Each labored breath and each pounding heartbeat reminded him how he'd softened in academic life.

He stopped suddenly. He bent over, hands on knees, gasping, ears ringing. He stayed bent over until the pain eased. He looked up, eyes blurred by perspiration, and saw Graham approach with the limber stride of a champion runner. He held the gasoline container like a baton.

'Out of shape, George,' Graham taunted. 'They sent you down here to check on me and you can't run to save your life. I bet he told you it would be an easy assignment, nothing dangerous. And you believed him.'

Graham stood his compact self a few feet away, arms akimbo, and took in the pathetically exhausted Mueller, the spent husk of a one-time college athlete.

'And you don't smoke, or drink. You have no excuse, George. The life of the mind has weakened your body. We're safe. We've gone far enough. The Land Rover is just ahead and we'll get on with the drive when I put in the gas. If it hasn't had its tires stripped.'

They approached the abandoned vehicle and quickly saw it had not been touched. It took three turns of the ignition to start the engine. They both took comfort in the engine's throaty cough. Mueller didn't turn on the headlights and put his hand on the gearshift.

'Take your hands off the steering wheel,' Graham said sharply. He nodded out the driver's-side window. Mueller saw shapes in the dark, and he knew suddenly they were surrounded by men who'd emerged from the culvert. Too many to count. Bearded men. Grim faces caked in dust, guns pointing at them.

'He's telling you to take your hands off the steering wheel,' Graham said again with urgency.

Mueller calculated the danger, the speed of the Land Rover, the cover of darkness. Then he complied, lifting his hands in surrender. A rebel with a Thompson submachine gun had taken up a position on the road in front of the Land Rover. In the rear view mirror Mueller saw a squad of men in fatigues approach. He saw a dozen men with guns on either side. He'd trained for this once, how to surrender to danger without surrendering to fear. His eye catalogued the arsenal. New M1 Garand rifles taken from Batista's surrendering forces, or bought from soldiers who'd deserted; a few old shotguns, one submachine gun, a bazooka, and one weapon that surprised him. The barrel of the assault rifle was trimmed with a muzzle sight. A Ceska semi-automatic weapon. Russian troops in Vienna preferred it to their own Kalashnikov, and it was a top barter item. It had the reputation of being a fine small arm – light, sturdy, and it fired twenty-five rounds a minute. The details of the weapon were fixed in Mueller's mind, like a sonnet committed to memory. He'd owned one.

Mueller saw the Czech pistol when the rebel pointed it through the window at his forehead. The man's face was angular, with a straggly untrimmed beard, and eyes wide and hostile. He wore a July 26th Movement armband.

'Hola, Americano.'

Mueller eyed the man's index finger, poised on the trigger.

Mueller met his eyes and saw his smile, mischievous with power. His front tooth was chipped. Mueller saw all of the man at once, trying to judge his jeopardy. A shifting knot of rebels surrounded the Land Rover, looking at the scene. Mueller heard the staccato rhythm of an urgent guttural Spanish from a hasty conference taking place among several of their captors. One rebel shouted into a walkie-talkie with a voice loud enough to rouse the countryside. *Urgente. Urgente.* No code. No caution, only the confusion of a night skirmish.

A commander arrived from somewhere and rebels circled him, greeting him, and then they parted to let him pass. He moved through the group and along the way he gave a bear hug, or shook a man's hand, or gave encouragement with a hand on a shoulder. He spoke to each man in a voice that was surprisingly soft, but distinct, nodding, or eyes growing large in recognition, and always his pleasant tenor greeting.

He was taller than the others, and he wore a cowboy hat that he'd tipped back on his head like a heartthrob cast in a Hollywood Western. He stood at the driver's window and pondered his two captives.

'You are Toby Graham.' He said the name phonetically, vowels stretched and accented. He looked at Mueller. 'I don't know you.' He lowered his head to address Graham. 'Come with me.'

A light rain had begun. Mueller found himself alone in the Land Rover, and the rebels had withdrawn and stood or sat in the roadside culvert under the protection of a leafy tree. Mueller had shut off the engine to conserve fuel, and he looked in the rear view mirror to the dark place where he'd seen Graham disappear in the company of the commander. Rebels didn't shoot American prisoners. He knew that. A hostage had more value than a corpse.

Mueller kept thinking about the Czech weapons, most likely guns from the stock made during World War II, which then entered the gray market of military weapons that armed insurgents around the world. Cash, clandestine transport, and local collaboration put them in the hands of political oppositions.

Mueller was startled when he heard the passenger door open. He'd drifted off in an uneasy sleep with his head slumped on the steering wheel. Graham slipped into the passenger seat. Mueller glanced in the rear view mirror and then to either side of the Land Rover. The rebels were gone.

'Let's go,' Graham said. 'Drive before they change their minds.'

Mueller stared at Graham. 'What?'

'What's not clear? We are free to go. Drive.'

'He knew you,' Mueller said. 'He knew your name. What is going on?'

A wall of water was moving across the savanna and the first gusts of wind brought rain that smacked the windshield. The hurricane's fury was upon them.

Graham nodded. His hand commanded Mueller to drive. 'Knavish speech sleeps in a fool's ear, George. Let's go. Now.'

5

HURRICANE

At dawn Mueller lay in a guestroom in Hacienda Madrigal with the wind howling outside. He and Graham had arrived as the hurricane hit, and any questions about what had kept them out were lost to the household's urgent storm preparations. No one had a moment to pull them aside and ask why they'd been delayed.

Electricity was knocked out first. Then the telephone. Transistor radios lost signal too. Mueller felt the crushing loneliness of the dark guestroom. Rain pelted the roof with the intensity of mad birds throwing themselves at the red tiles. It was too much to be alone. In time, he made his way through the storm's murky darkness with a whiskey bottle sprouting a lit candle and joined the small community in the living room gathered around wicked storm lamps. Mueller felt helpless in the midst of Jack's heroic effort to coax a prize bull into the barn against the wind's fury, his help waved off, so he'd joined the other guests. Liz politely declined his offer to help Maximo, the caretaker, take inventory of candles, flashlights, foodstuffs, and potable water. The loyal servant, a runty man with a limp, claimed his authority over the tasks with grandiose confidence. 'He came with the house,' Liz whispered. 'He grew up here. It's more his house than ours.' She pointed to a large rug on the living room floor and announced to the room, 'There is a storm cellar if we need it.'

Mueller was among a few neighbors with homes close to the flood-prone river who sought shelter in Hacienda Madrigal. A few Americans, he saw. Katie was there, but when he looked again she was gone, and no one saw her leave. Graham? Among the small group there was a certain nervous pleasure and false sense of excitement. At the time, Mueller was unable to formulate this assessment – it only came to him later, thinking in retrospect – nonetheless, he felt it in the mood in the room, and he sensed it in the curious defiant way that the guests willed themselves to have a good time. It was this oblique feeling that Mueller began to sense was the worried giddiness of strangers brought together by looming jeopardy.

The conversation came out of nowhere. Mueller was talking to the wife of an ITT executive, a big woman dressed boldly in tennis whites for a garden party, who had insisted on addressing Mueller as professor, and extracted information on New Haven with intense questions that came in clipped staccato rhythm, and Mueller knew that nothing short of rudeness was going to save him from her inquisition – so when he heard his name called from behind he was quick to shift his attention.

'You're George Mueller, aren't you?'

Mueller looked at an Englishman he'd seen earlier when he entered the room. Tall man, thin, droopy eyelids, and a lazy shock of hair that he repeatedly pushed off his forehead. Younger side of middle age. Mueller, whose eyes had barely scanned the room when he entered, had, however, been drawn to this man alone with cards playing solitaire, and from there he had noticed the man rise to look out the front door when wind tore a branch off a tree. The man sat alone, not thinking to introduce himself, and no one spoke to him. The mood wasn't convivial and there was no occasion for anyone in the circumstantial community to go out of his way to be polite. Mueller at one point had turned an eye toward the Englishman and he'd seen a change. He had risen and proposed cocktails to the group. Although he'd been quiet much of the morning, the prospect of alcohol revived the man. He took his gin without olive or vermouth, but still called it a martini. He went from quiet solitude to restless talker in the space of two draughts of gin, and then he toasted the group. 'To humor that endures the storm.'

And now he faced Mueller – eyes bright – and he repeated Mueller's name, louder, as if he thought he hadn't been heard, but of course Mueller had heard him.

'Am I interrupting?' he asked.

Mueller took in the man – a blush of gin on his rosy cheeks. He wore white cotton pants, white laced shoes, a cream cable knit sweater, fully two pounds of sagging fabric.

'I think we're finished,' Mueller said, offering the wife of the ITT executive a courtly nod.

'I'm Phillip Callingwood. Exciting times. My first hurricane.' The man's eyes cast about the now morose guests who slumped in chairs, or picked at the food Liz had put out. Fruit, bread and butter, melting. Crackers. The half-dozen people had formed intimate groups of two or three to brave the storm's claustrophobia. He offered his hand. 'I work for the *London Times*. Their man in Cuba.'

Mueller gripped the offered hand, but he found it limp. 'Calloway, you said.'

'Callingwood. English, not Irish.'

'Of course.'

Callingwood lifted his chin and eyed Mueller. 'You know, the days of you Americans treating Cuba as a recreational junket for gambling and sex is about to end.' His eyes grew wide and he added, 'Batista is stumbling badly to a violent end.'

Callingwood sipped his depleted drink. He spoke tartly. 'Tell me, is there a distinction between a man who applies electrodes to a prisoner's genitals and the man in Washington who sits behind his desk and pretends he doesn't know it's happening, although he knows very well that he paid for the battery?'

Mueller knew all at once what he disliked about Callingwood. He personified the category of Englishman living overseas who clung with affected smugness to colonial prejudices, precious in his manner, sardonic, alcoholic – who thought everyone else, but especially the Americans, inferior.

'That's an odd question,' Mueller said.

'Odd? Why odd?'

'You seem to know the answer.'

'Look,' Callingwood said. He drew closer. 'You Americans are bungling this arms embargo. You excoriate Batista for turning guns on civilians, but you're doing nothing to get rid of him. You pay lip service to democracy here.' Callingwood leaned into Mueller with his gin breath and said smugly, 'Hypocrisy, sir, a vice dressed up as a virtue.'

In the dark archive of his mind that stored resentments Mueller remembered his editor's comment – *crumbling cold water castles not fit to sleep in.* Mueller smiled benignly. He took a step back from Callingwood, but found the Englishman, now engaged, had more to say.

'You're a friend of that fellow, Toby Graham. Is he here?' The Englishman's eyes came back to Mueller. 'Any truth to the rumors?'

Everyone had a rumor on Graham. Mueller didn't react.

'Works for the CIA,' Callingwood said.

'That's what they say about every American who doesn't have a good story.'

'Is he?'

'If I knew I wouldn't tell you. If I said he wasn't, you wouldn't believe me.'

'It's well known.'

Mueller scoffed. 'The only thing well known about Toby Graham is that he isn't well known.'

Callingwood smiled. 'So, I haven't shocked you. You don't look like someone who is easily shocked. Join us in a game of rummy?'

Mueller had no interest in a game of cards, but he was happy to use the invitation to escape further conversation with his female interrogator. Callingwood was the only one in the group with his heart in the game, and when a thoughtless error was made in the order of play he got irritated. A third gin martini helped him accept the indifference of the group's play, and he took to talking, compelled by the others' silence.

'It's strange and violent weather,' he said. 'These hurricanes. I have seen tempests' winds fell the knotty oak and I have seen ambitious oceans swell and rage and foam, but never until tonight, never until now with you, did I feel the strife of a card game like this.'

That got the others to look at him, but they thought he was drunk so they carried on with their indifferent play.

The wife of the United Fruit executive looked up from her cards and spoke to the woman opposite, the president of the Camaguey Tennis Club.

'The Bancrofts left. And the Baileys. Luis and Bella Fulup opted to fly to Minneapolis last week and left their place minded by a caretaker. Helen Longanecker was recalled by the Baptist ministry. The Louis Jeffrey Millers are gone. And the Victor Rankens and the Harold Pitts, with their retrievers, on a plane sent by his company. You can't get a ticket out on a commercial airline. They've stopped flying. The rebels control the approach and they have threatened to send up rockets at any aircraft that tries to land. Unless you have your own airplane I'm afraid you're stuck.'

The woman threw down a card. 'There is a rumor the embassy has arranged to send a plane, but I don't believe it. They have become useless.'

She looked around the table. 'Have any of you seen the William Andersens? Or the teacher Dorothy Whitten? Have they gone too?' She took a card from the discard pile. 'Well, things will work out. We do a service here that they need. Who is going to run the telephones when my husband leaves? We do have a role to play. Even communists need telephones.'

Mueller smiled tolerantly. He took the opportunity to excuse himself and then with a borrowed flashlight made his way upstairs to his room. He still hadn't seen Katie, but he'd seen Graham outside lending a hand at the hard work of trying to close a storm shutter torn loose by the wind.

Mueller lay on his bed and stared at the ceiling. He flicked the flashlight on and off, and then when that bored him, he lay in the dark and listened to the howling wind and lashing rain. He lay that way for a long time, thoughts drifting, the end of one becoming the start of another.

At one point Mueller rose and opened his journal. The desk faced the shuttered window and he illuminated the pages with his whiskey candle. He picked up his pen, listened to the wind, forming a thought. He wanted to capture some of his impressions of the darkened day in the event he could find a way to weave the storm's drama into his travel piece. Then it struck him that little, perhaps nothing, of what he'd so far experienced in Cuba was suitable for his editor's assignment.

His thoughts drifted. He went back over the story. The detail of the assault rifle and its Czech origin kept him from feeling tired. He began to see there was a way to think about Graham's life as spun from a single filament of fact woven loosely into a fabric of sheer audacity. His mind returned to the spy's world of reasoning that calibrated everything – hope, despair, loyalty, trust. His thoughts swirled, keeping him from rest, and he felt the terrible confinement of his room.

Mueller walked to the end of the hall and wandered the house until he found himself in the library. Tall shelves of old books called out with their histories, distracting him. Suddenly, he was aware that he was not alone. He turned and saw a woman at a window looking out at the dark shape of the wind-bent *algarrobo* tree, standing perfectly still, meditating or praying. The howling wind was muffled by the glass.

'Liz?'

He had startled her.

'Everything okay?'

A pause. 'No, everything is not okay.'

Mueller was at her side.

She looked at her hands. 'I am afraid of what will happen here. Can there be a good ending?'

They stood side by side, faces dimly lit in the flickering storm lamp. Mueller felt their hearts bonded by the sadness she carried, which made him tolerant of her long silence.

'This is what you want to know.' She turned suddenly to him, placid eyes alive. 'Toby followed me here.' And then words tumbled out. 'Somehow he learned my address. I didn't know what to think at first. He showed up the day after we met in the Nacional. I had gone back to leave you a message and there he was in the hotel lobby. I didn't know what to think. I was stunned, then angry. He could see that. I had pushed so hard to get him out of my mind. All that hard work for nothing. It has been four years. The world changes – my world changed.'

She took a breath. 'I agreed to see him that evening. What choice did I have? We walked along the Malecon and suddenly Havana at dusk looked heartbreakingly beautiful. We strolled along the seawall cooled by the mist from the crashing waves. There were a few laughing couples, but we had the evening to ourselves. He didn't have a plan, nor did I, but when we saw a small restaurant we went in. There were only a few tables. I remember the smell of the sea air. All my senses were heightened and each moment came to me and lingered. We sat on the patio and the breeze swept away the mosquitoes. I was too nervous to be interested in food. After all, it had been four years since I'd seen him – and I didn't look at the menu. Nor did he. When the waiter arrived, he ordered a drink and I had a Coke. Alcohol would make me say or do something I'd regret.

'We ordered food not because we were hungry but because dining gave us time to stretch the evening, and when the food arrived I hardly touched mine. He was gentlemanly and apologetic and he gave me some crazy story about why he'd come – something about the days we'd spent together and how he was different – better. *Changed.* I felt a panic and I looked around. I was afraid we'd be seen by someone I knew and then I'd have to lie about why I was there. He saw me and said, "No one will know me." I replied, "But they will know *me*."'

'It was a strange conversation, one of those moments in life that you dream about, and when it does happen you are unprepared. He asked me why I hadn't said goodbye in Guatemala, or left my address. I told him he was out of danger. The wound had healed and he didn't need me. He was asleep when I left, I said, and I didn't want to disturb him. It was a lie and I don't think he believed the lie. I wasn't ready to accept that he had come back into my life. I am thirty-six years old, for God's sake. I'm married. I've built a life here. Is it perfect? No, but I'm not ready to throw it away on a romantic impulse.'

The storm had strengthened as the day grew late, and the howling wind drew Mueller and Liz closer. The jeopardy of the moment deepened and turned profound. Smells of rain drifted to them and branches ripped from trunks flew into the air. A woman with wounded memories finds it helpful to succor the pain by sharing thoughts with a friend. And so it happened.

Liz led Mueller to a leather couch in the middle of the room.

'I've never told this to anyone, but it's time. I want you to know. You of all people should know. For whatever happens.'

Liz described how she'd met Graham while traveling from Guatemala City north through the mountains. Jack, she said, was attending an agricultural summit sponsored by the State Department. She found the speeches boring, the participants a dull crowd of ranchers and corporate farmers, so she took a long weekend trip alone to the ruins at Zaculeu. She traveled by bus from Quetzaltenango and during the trip the axle broke, stranding passengers. Toby happened to drive by in a jeep. She was the only American among the passengers and he offered a lift.

The jeep lurched and bounced on the curving mountain road and she was tossed around. The proximity of their bodies made her jittery – alone with a stranger. She remembered being thrown into his lap and she remembered too there was music coming from the jeep's radio. She apologized for the contact, acknowledging to Mueller her impulse to apologize for things that weren't at all her fault. His reply was among his first words in what was to become an animated conversation between two people sharing a ride in a remote place – life stories coming out between strangers.

'Truthfully,' she said, 'I liked the idea of visiting the Mayan ruins, but I also wanted to get away from Jack. Toby and I just hit it off, and I saw all these things in him that I didn't see in Jack – or hadn't seen in a long time. I was trapped in my marriage and this drive in the mountains with this handsome, quiet man was a pleasant diversion. Jack had wanted me to accompany him on his business trip and then he abandoned me, so I went off on my own little adventure.'

She paused. 'I remember what he was wearing: khaki pants, a rumpled short-sleeve shirt, his arms tan, and he was lean from heat and work. He gripped the steering wheel and I remember thinking he had strong hands – hands without calluses – and I wondered how he had come to be driving the Guatemalan mountains that day. After all, it was the middle of nowhere. We both laughed at the coincidence. It was a long ride and I found myself, and I think he did too, surprised at the ease with which we openly talked about ourselves – our past, our hopes, our sadness, our yearning. All things I wouldn't dare say to a close friend, but I could say to a stranger because there was no consequence. We would come to our destination and go our separate ways – never to see each other again.'

She looked at Mueller. 'It's happened to you, I'm sure. It happens to everyone.'

She turned the red string bracelet on her wrist, lost in thought. She lifted her eyes. 'Two hours into the drive we were sideswiped by a speeding bus on a narrow curve. I remember one moment there was music on the radio and then a deafening crash. The sudden explosion rang in my ears for hours. I opened my eyes and saw the jeep had gone off the road and tilted against a wood guard rail. Through the window I saw we were hung up on a post over the edge of a wide embankment that dropped sharply to a gorge. We knew those seconds might be the last seconds of our lives. The crash removed any hint of formality between us. Possibly because of the intimate conversation we had shared, my only thought was that our lives had been entangled in some previous life, and that we were meant to die together. That thought came and went in a flash, but in the moment it was pure. We were connected in a way that I had never connected with a man. We were, in my mind, alive, then dead, then alive again. I knew that something had changed between us. The intimacy of death brought us close. There was no room for fear; moreover, the thought I might die in that remote spot was overwhelming.'

The jeep, she said, had tipped from its perch and suddenly rolled down the embankment. It turned over and over on the slope, and her only thought as the jeep approached the gorge's edge was, again, that they were fated to die together.

'Yes, as strange as it may sound, that notion created a bond.

The thought calmed me like a giant hand placed on my forehead, quieting the fear. And in the moment it seemed inevitable.

'It was okay. This was my time to die, I thought.' She paused. 'The jeep continued to tumble down through snapping branches until it came to an abrupt rest. It had propped against a tree at the precipice, and hundreds of feet below was the river. Everything was quiet except for the rapids. It was chaotic in the jeep. Bags and luggage were thrown around. I didn't hear him. There was only the sound of a spinning tire, and beyond that, deep in the gorge, rushing water.

'I called his name. He wasn't in the driver's seat. I managed to extract myself from the vehicle when the metal groaned. There was a loud snap, like a whip, and the jeep fell to the river. The whoosh of the jeep falling ended when it hit the rocks. I was shaking. I was left feeling alive, but empty.

'For a moment I thought Toby was in the jeep and that I had survived and he had not. I found him on the slope just below the road where he'd been thrown, unconscious. I was paralyzed for a moment, happy he was alive, then overwhelmed by a responsibility to get help. He had a terrible gash on his forehead.

'I stopped a passing truck and the driver took us to Quetzaltenango. There was a small hotel and I got him into a bed with the driver's help. There was no hospital and the local clinic was closed. I found a French doctor from an archeological expedition who came to the hotel and stitched the gash on Toby's head, and an arm wound. He referred to Toby as my husband because that was how I had registered us, and I didn't correct him.

'I stayed with Toby five days. He had a high fever the first night and I stayed up and cooled him with a wet cloth. When he finally drifted off I saw his canvas bag, which the driver had retrieved from the slope. Inside I found a pistol, maps, and a radio.

'I asked him about the things the next morning, when the fever passed. He admitted little of what he did – I assumed it was little, and that there was much more to his story than he let on, but I didn't ask further. I nursed him and in those days and nights I found myself close to him.'

Liz looked at Mueller. 'You could say I found myself drawn to him. Caring for him, cooling his fever, and when he was healthy, we became lovers. It was startling and frightening. I woke on the fifth morning and realized it was a mistake. I left early at dawn the next day while he slept. I left a note.'

She looked down at the bracelet, one hand turning the string round and round. She looked up at Mueller, eyes defiant. 'I was married. I wasn't ready to give up my life. I was frightened of the work he did. The coup was in all the newspapers.'

'So,' she said, 'that's what happened. I left him there. I didn't give an address and I didn't ask for his, but he had my name. It's what one does when one is disoriented. I was disoriented, although at the time I didn't know it. I thought I was being responsible. Toby was present in my thoughts the next years, but each day a little less. You could say I'd begun to forget him. I lost track of his presence in my past as if the incident only had consequence when it happened. Packed away in an archive of my heart. I picked up my life where it had left off. I met Jack in Guatemala City and life went on. I told Jack nothing.'

Liz paused. 'I kept it from him because we weren't intimate then. I hid everything. I made up a visit to the Mayan ruins. I lied about being out of touch.' She touched the bracelet. 'I lied about this. Toby gave it to me. I kept it to remind me of what happened. In the months that followed I forgot about Toby, but then without warning he'd pop into my mind when a jeep passed, or I saw a man similar in build on the street, or when I read about Guatemala in the newspaper.'

Liz let out an anguished laugh. 'In a way it always seemed inevitable that one day he would show up in Havana. Then he did.'

Liz explained that she had received a letter from Graham six months after the accident, but she had not answered it. She placed it in a locked jewelry box and occasionally she had unfolded it, flattening the edges, and read the plea by the man who had briefly blazed into her life.

'That's it,' Liz said. She stood abruptly. 'Now you know.'

6

RECKONING

'You're sure?' Pryce asked.

Mueller sat across a gray metal conference table and watched the FBI agent contemplate the smoke that rose from the cigarette he held with two fingers. The ash had lengthened and he tapped the end into his coffee cup. He brought his eyes back to Mueller and waited for an answer.

'I'm sure.' Mueller felt the claustrophobia of the U.S. Embassy's top-floor conference room. No windows. No sense of day or night. The freezing air-conditioning made the meeting seem unnatural. He had flown out from the damaged airstrip after a weeklong effort removed downed trees and repaired holes left by the receding flood waters.

'You don't sound sure.'

'Maybe you don't believe me.'

'Oh, I believe you. I want to believe you. But I hear doubt in your voice. Maybe you don't want to be certain.'

'Twice he was called the Americano. I know what I heard and I know what I saw.' Mueller repeated his account of Graham's disappearance with the rebels, giving the facts as he remembered them, consulting his notes. He recalled how Graham had returned as if nothing had happened and he repeated Graham's witty brush-off. Mueller gave what he knew – the garrison asleep, the call of the bird – or was it a signal? Their lucky escape moments before the attack.

'He knew something was going to happen,' Mueller said. 'It was not a coincidence that we got out in time.'

The two men looked at each other. Pryce's fingers tapped the table in a slow drum roll. 'I suppose I should be more surprised – or maybe impressed. A coup is what you'd expect of him – what I expected – but it was a magician's trick.' He saw he had confused Mueller. 'The hand draws attention to itself, but the real action is elsewhere. He was happy to have me think the rifles were to arm a coup. But you didn't believe that, did you? He's capable of anything, but not incompetence.' Pryce laughed. He ground his cigarette in the saucer. He looked at Mueller. 'Did you know this all along?'

Mueller felt the question like an accusation. A cop's mentality. Everyone a suspect.

There was a long silence. Pryce let his eyes drift back to Mueller.

'Here's what I see. He's put guns in the hands of the rebels. You saw the Czech weapons. You don't get those from Army deserters. He is off the reservation, fed up with official policy, making up his own. You will put it more elegantly, but that's what I see.'

Mueller acknowledged the logic, seduced by it, but he was also repelled. He asked himself again, but with a different emphasis, would a thirty-seven-year-old officer of the CIA earmarked for great things commit an act of treason so outrageous that if detected it could cost him his career, his freedom, indeed his life? Namely, delivering guns in breach of the embargo into the hands of the rebels? The thought rankled with Mueller – astonished him really – but there it was. That's what he was being asked to believe. Mueller knew no paymaster controlled Graham. No Soviet puppeteer plucked the strings that made him dance. He was confident of that. Soviets in Cuba? Toby Graham turned? No. Mueller could only believe, if he believed Pryce at all, and he wasn't sure how much of what Pryce said was true and how much invented to promote the FBI's stubbornly simple-minded view of itself, that Graham was acting on his own.

'You've made your judgment. That's it?'

'There's a war on. Men are dying with guns he's brought in.'

'You're rushing to judgment.'

'He knows very well what he is doing.'

Mueller knew that he was seeing the real Frank Pryce, the loyal operator following Washington's orders. A poke in the eye. Mueller felt Pryce stare coldly and he had the uncomfortable sensation that the man across the table was judging him, trying to peer into his mind.

Pryce leaned forward. 'His treason is fresh and speed must answer it.'

Mueller felt Pryce's remark like a rope around Graham's neck. 'More evidence would help,' he snapped. He stared at Pryce. 'We're talking about a man's life here.'

Mueller got his answer in Pryce's long silence and his flat expression. There was no further discussion, no instructions, no plan, but the next step was clear enough to Mueller. When evil raised its head it always seemed to do so with great clarity.

Only the pursuit of justice, or the excavation of truth, required a nuanced imagination – and a ponderous study of evidence.

'There's nothing you can do,' Pryce said. 'You've played your part and it didn't help. I wanted to believe Graham was following orders – then I'd be able to protect him.' He paused. 'Alonzo has suspected this for some time. I had to keep him from acting. I can't do that any longer. Here's what will happen next. Graham will be in a café in Camaguey. Perhaps in the company of a SIM agent who is posing as a member of the July 26th Movement. A green Oldsmobile will drive up. Graham might be arrested. More likely he will be assassinated. This is how things are done in Cuba. The circumstances might be different, but the treachery will be the same. The outcome identical. Only the time is uncertain.'

Mueller's mind was calm. 'When?'

Pryce knitted his brow. His fingers had taken up their impatient tapping. 'A week. Two. Three on the outside. They don't need to be sophisticated about this. A man and a gun. Executioners are easy to hire.' Pryce met Mueller's eyes. 'Does he trust you?'

'He doesn't trust anyone.'

'Will he listen to you?'

'It depends on what I say. Will he leave if I tell him his life is at risk?' Mueller laughed. 'That adrenaline is his heroin.'

Pryce smiled. 'Let's go. There is someone we need to visit.'

*

Mueller looked out the Packard's rear window to see if he recognized where the driver had stopped. The grand Beaux Arts apartment house was in a line of nineteenth-century buildings that graced El Paseo del Prado, empty at that late hour. Across the harbor channel El Morro was brilliantly illuminated for the night. Mueller slid across the backseat and followed Pryce onto the sidewalk, nodding at the driver, who held open the rear door. Mueller couldn't read anything into the man's expression.

Mickey Ruden was suddenly there talking to the driver. 'Keep an eye open. Check the street, the lobby, the sidewalk. And don't bring attention. Make it look casual. If you see something suspicious, something that doesn't check out, you ring the apartment bell twice. Start the car. Keep the engine running until we come down. Do you understand?'

Mueller and Pryce followed Ruden into the ornate lobby. A wide marble staircase with Art Nouveau banister spiraled up four floors to a leaded-glass skylight. It reminded Mueller of the luxury homes in Vienna – the grandeur, the privacy, the quiet. How quickly one became aware of silence in so boisterous a city as Havana. Mueller had reached the second floor when he became convinced that he was making a mistake. His instinct for danger rose in the uncomfortable silence as he entered the unfamiliar place. They reached the third floor, where a woman held open a door and suddenly any reasonable excuse to turn back was gone.

The woman ushered them in, and when they passed her, she looked quickly down at the lobby. Satisfied, she closed the door and locked it. He saw she was young and pretty, with curly black hair that fell to her shoulders. She had olive skin and long delicate fingers, the hands of a pianist. Ruden had walked by her without acknowledging her. Mueller saw she was reserved, quiet, and mindful of the men. Ruden's nod was her instruction, and the Cuban mistress disappeared into another room. Mueller knew, as did everyone, that Ruden's wife and daughter lived in Miami.

'She is discreet,' Ruden said when he saw Mueller look where the woman had gone. 'Drink?' Ruden moved across the room to a tall glass breakfront with bottles. Mueller followed, his eyes taking in the oil paintings of a bucolic medieval Rome. Fabric covered the walls and French doors were thrown open to the night. Somewhere in the distance the cry of a baby.

Ruden poured Pryce a scotch on the rocks without asking a preference. Mueller thought, *Well acquainted.* Ruden's eyes solicited Mueller's request.

'Club soda.'

He poured Mueller a glass. 'Ice?' He took his own drink of chocolate liqueur in crystal. 'Frank says you have a situation. I might be of help.'

Mueller looked at Pryce.

'Am I wrong?' Ruden asked. 'Is it not why you're here?'

'I filled him in,' Pryce said to Mueller, speaking as if they were alone and not standing beside Ruden. 'He doesn't know everything, but he knows enough. Let's hear what he has to say.'

Later, Mueller would remember the mobster's smile – pleasant and polite with a vague anguish that drew sympathy. There was no cost to hear him out. The three men stood in a tight group in the middle of the room, and it was only when Ruden began to ramble on about an unrelated topic that Mueller became conscious how none of them had moved to the sofas.

'Havana has everything to make me happy,' Ruden was saying. 'Everything but one thing. The chickens. You can't get a decent chicken. They are all skinny and tough. But it's a great place if you don't eat chickens. Beef is no problem. We serve the best steaks in my hotels. Seafood is good, which you'd expect.

Pork is first class. But fresh chicken is the problem. The local ones are scrawny. We have to fly chickens in from Tampa. As I said, Havana has everything to make me happy. We don't like trouble and sometimes opportunity comes along dressed up like a good looking hooker and you're not sure what to do.'

He sipped his chocolate liqueur. He nodded at Pryce and then at Mueller. 'We have good relations with Batista. The only problem we have – except for the chickens – is that he is losing the war. Every month we meet with him and he wants more. The more his army loses the more he wants in his palm. That's the only problem. We can bring in chickens, but we can't stop the defeats. You know what I mean.' Ruden turned the crystal in his hand. 'You admire the glass?' he said to Mueller. 'It's Murano.'

Ruden nudged Mueller to the open French doors. 'Here, let me show you.' Beyond the gleaming dome of the Presidential Palace a modern glass building rose above the skyline. 'The new Hilton makes all the difference. The name is known everywhere. We want to make Havana the Monte Carlo of the Caribbean.'

Cool evening air came in from the sea and refreshed the stale room air.

'We don't like the revolution. It's hard for tourists to relax when there's violence in the streets. I understand this man Toby Graham is putting guns in the hands of the rebels. It's in our mutual interest to handle him the right way. He is your friend. That's important. I respect that. SIM agents know what he does. They only know one solution, which is not the solution I would want.'

Ruden paused. 'Let me tell you a story. I had a home in the States with woodchucks. My wife liked them. They are little furry animals that sit on the lawn and our daughter liked to look out the window when they ate the dandelions. They're cute, but they dig burrows under the house, and these burrows undermined the foundation. It was going to crack. A big problem, these little cute animals. I had to get rid of them, but I knew I'd break my wife's heart if I used a kill trap. So I did it humanely. I had them trapped and set free in a nature preserve.' Ruden looked at Mueller. 'That's what we need to do here. No one gets hurt, but we remove the problem.'

The meeting ended. A few details would follow, Ruden said, but the plan was set. All that remained was to bait the trap.

'Bit of a shook,' Pryce said when they were outside on the sidewalk. El Paseo del Prado was empty in both directions except for the Packard and the driver, who nodded. 'A kind gesture from the likes of him.'

'You believe him?' Mueller asked.

'Graham dead? That's not good for Ruden. Alonzo would be blamed and it would alarm Washington. Things become uncertain. It's better for business if Graham goes quietly.'

Mueller pondered. 'I need a drink. Where will they take him?'

'Where he can walk barefoot on ice thinking of summer's heat.' Pryce winked.

Mueller and Pryce stepped out of El Floridita after an hour of cautious drinking – careful to stay sober in each other's company. Pryce turned back the whistled solicitations of two prostitutes who approached from across the street. Pryce was a cop, a professional, even on his own time. Mueller remembered Graham's comment. *He doesn't know how to dance.* Mueller felt the weight of what had been settled that night, but in coming to a settlement, still nothing seemed as it should be. This was not how he thought things would turn out. What he'd thought was true was no longer true. Then the elemental fear of being wrong came over him, and he felt daunted. Something wasn't right. He remembered how the director had boasted the CIA and FBI had gotten over the old rivalries. *If there is a success they can take credit and we won't have to dirty our hands.* Mueller pondered the words and he remembered how unpersuasively they had been said.

Mueller and Pryce were walking in silence – two men joined in conspiracy but not enjoying trust – when Pryce suddenly stopped. They had come to the USS *Maine* memorial that honored dead American sailors killed when the cruiser exploded in Havana harbor in 1898. Pryce contemplated the tall marble columns, refulgent in moonlight, and the bronze eagle with its wings spread wide, talons clawing the globe. The busts of Roosevelt and McKinley graced the huge stone monument and were a reminder of an earlier war.

'We honor our dead,' Pryce said. 'A terrible tragedy. Threequarters of its crew killed. Good men. All the tabloids ran big headlines. There was public outrage across America. McKinley had no choice but to invade. Today's Washington politicians are bleating cowards.' Pryce spat his contempt. 'The whole lot of them are wishy-washy, whiny, and weak. We need another Teddy Roosevelt here. Another *Maine*.'

Not since West Berlin, when his colleagues advocated for harsh interrogations in which the subject might die, had Mueller felt such revulsion. There was no one at the memorial to see a solitary man stare appalled at his colleague.

7

ALL SAINTS' WEEK

PERFECT WEATHER AT THE start of All Saints' Week provided the opportunity to honor the promise of the day. Clear sky. Warm sun. Pleasant breeze from the north. It was agreed by everyone that Camaguey's streets would be packed with a holiday crowd and they should avoid town and head to the beach. A day of rest and relaxation was what they all needed to get away from continuously grim war news.

Katie too joined the group, having gone missing during the hurricane, and everyone worried she'd been swept away in the flood waters. But she had reappeared a few days later after telephone service was restored, brought into Hacienda Madrigal on an oxcart. She wore a bright, ambitious smile, muddy fatigues, and her Leica camera. She hopped off the cart into Liz's embrace as the household emptied to greet her. The excitement of her safe return stilled the previous week's urgency to get her on a plane to Miami. Crises followed crises and the best protection against expulsion, or arrest, was the continuous unfolding of events, each more urgent than the last, that preoccupied the police.

The beach was blustery, the breeze too chilly for sunbathing, but they were not willing to concede disappointment in the face of their high expectations of a beach picnic, so they endured the weather, making fun of themselves. When they'd spent enough time in misery to justify the hour drive, they packed up and headed back to Hacienda Madrigal.

Two vehicles had taken the group out and brought the four of them home. Liz insisted that Mueller join her in the Land Rover on the return, which left Katie to go with Jack in his pickup. 'Oh, he's not so bad,' Liz whispered to Katie. 'He likes you. Let him tell you all about the tick problem. You won't have to say a word.'

Mueller's vivid memory of the ride back was of sitting in the passenger seat staring at the red dust cloud mushrooming a mile ahead. The road was pitted and dry and Jack's pickup was the only vehicle visible. 'He likes the pickup on these roads,' Liz said to Mueller. 'He likes to bounce around. It makes him feel like he's in Texas.' She laughed sadly.

Mueller glanced at her.

Liz threw out: 'Jack invited Toby for dinner tonight.' She turned to Mueller. 'I wish he hadn't done that.' She looked straight ahead at the dust mushrooming behind the pickup. 'I wish Toby hadn't come. I have a life here and now he's shown up.'

Mueller waited for her to finish her complaint.

'We never go to the beach here,' she said. 'Strange, don't you think? All these tourists pay through the nose for vacations to the beaches that we could visit any day of the week. And we don't. You don't see many Cubans at the beaches or in the water. If you think about it, sunbathing is a sort of madness – to lie on hot sand and sunburn. Have you ever seen fishermen sunbathe? Or an Arab? Well, that's the point. It's a madness of the idle rich.'

They had gone halfway and the channels of choppy water that lined the coast road had given way to dry burnt savannah. High cirrus clouds sailed across a chalk blue sky. Suddenly, Mueller heard Liz expel her exasperation.

'What does he want from me?'

'Who?'

'Toby. We are talking about Toby.'

'I didn't know we were talking about anyone.'

'We were talking about him a moment ago. I said I wished he hadn't come.' She looked at Mueller. 'What does he want from me?'

Mueller considered what not to say.

'Whatever it is it's too late,' she said. 'Jack and I have a life here. I am invested in it.' She had grasped the steering wheel and her knuckles had gone white.

'I don't mean to make it sound like a commercial enterprise with Jack – but it's a partnership. I don't forgive him his affairs, but I put up with them, yes. I tolerate them because we have this complicated life together. And I believe in the work I do here. I make a difference in the lives of the families we employ. Small things – food, clothing, medicine, and money if they need it. They are poor and we have means. I get satisfaction out of that. You might not understand.'

Her voice softened. 'What Jack gets from that girl? I know what it is. Let's settle that. I do know. He needs it so he takes it. He is an entitled man who wears no shame. I know this, but it took too long to see.'

She gazed ahead at Jack's pickup shrouded in a dust cloud. 'I use him as much as he uses the marriage. You didn't know that either. At my request, he has given title of small plots to the *precaristas* we employ. He has done that because I asked him to.'

She paused. Concern riveted her face. 'Don't judge this marriage, George.' She glanced sideways at him. 'It's easy to look at me and think I'm rationalizing a bad choice. Maybe I am.'

'Are you? Your heart doesn't seem to be in it.'

She cocked her head and tossed her hair. 'That's an odd word for you to use. I didn't know *heart* was in your vocabulary. It's not a word I expect to hear from you.'

'Why not?'

'It's not how I think of men like you. The work you do. Or did. Have you really gotten out? And now you teach bloody Shakespeare.' She laughed. It was a brittle laugh. 'I'm sorry.' Her face flushed and her arms collapsed over the steering wheel.

Mueller watched her agitated state. She maneuvered the Land Rover around potholes deepened by the hurricane. He was aware that she was driving faster than she should, swerving to avoid the perils, and she took one sharp bend in the road at high speed. A Brahman bull stood in the middle of the road. Liz honked but the large, stubborn animal lifted its head without concern. Liz brought the Land Rover to a skidding stop a few feet from his horns.

She opened her eyes and breathed deeply. The bull flicked its tail and remained in front of the Land Rover as an obstinate roadblock. Mueller opened his window and threw a stone. The bull kicked up a hind leg and lumbered off.

'Thank you, George. It almost killed us.'

'I had nothing to do with it. He spotted a cow in the field over there.'

Liz laughed. She had been driving a short distance when she turned to him. 'I'm sorry I called you heartless. Sometimes I think Jack wishes he'd gone into your line of work. Ranching bores him now.' Her voice drifted. 'He finds other distractions. He won't admit it, but the idea of Cuba changing excites him. He is good at bribes, but he is tired of them. Like he is tired of me.'

She was driving fast again, having allowed her foot to get heavy on the gas, and the Land Rover sped along. Mueller was uncomfortable with her mix of fraught emotion and reckless driving, and he gripped the handhold to keep his head from bouncing against the roof. 'You're going too fast, Liz.'

'Am I? Sorry.'

Liz braked, bringing the Land Rover to a sudden stop. Her shoulders shook and there came one convulsive heave that racked her chest. She stayed that way for a long moment – righteous weeping – and then it passed. She composed herself. Her brave face was streaked with tears and her cheeks flushed, but her eyes were fixed and determined.

Mueller placed a hand on her shoulder. He didn't say anything, nor did he know what to say. It took a special kind of person with a giving heart to offer sympathy, and he thought, yes, she was right. He didn't have that type of heart.

'I mean it. I'm sorry,' she said. 'I didn't mean to call you heartless.' She looked at him. 'How many sorrys is that? I always say I'm sorry and sometimes I say I'm sorry when it's the other person who is at fault, but to say I'm sorry is my way of dealing with things. Apologizing for other people's mistakes. I am too empathetic and you, I think, not enough.'

She looked at Mueller. 'I know you mean well. I couldn't be you. I wouldn't want to be someone who was numb to the misery around her, able to ignore what I saw.'

'Better to be you than me,' he said.

'Men are so *stuck*.' She snapped the word.

There was a beat of silence. 'Don't repeat any of this to Jack. It would only confuse him. And of course, you can't say anything to Toby. Do I have your word?'

Mueller gazed at her. He considered whether to offer advice, but that would require he reveal an alarming detail. He had no answers for what would surely be her urgent questions, so he nodded, but said nothing.

'Everything seems to be coming undone at the same time,' she said. 'My marriage. This life.' She turned to Mueller, eyes diverted from the road, and said fiercely, 'I don't love Toby.'

Mueller looked at her. *Be careful.* 'Of course you don't. How could you.'

'What was between us could not endure. Affection like that happens in one moment in a time and a place – like a Christmas globe with snowflakes – but that magic isn't life. This is life.' Her hand waved at Hacienda Madrigal's front gate and the tall palms that lined the driveway approach to the home. Jack's pickup was parked in front. 'My home.'

Mueller thought he heard her sarcasm incorrectly, but when he looked to confirm, she was already talking over her comment.

'I have a duty to all this and an obligation. The only thing I don't have is a child. That would seal the contract, wouldn't it? You put up with a lot to protect a child. But I have all this.' She waved her hand across Jack's pickup, rusted machinery at the barn, unweeded gardens gone to seed, a hammock strung between two trees, and the crumbling brow of the main house. 'This stuff.'

She looked at Mueller. 'Dinner is in an hour. What will you do now?'

'Write, I suppose. I've pushed off the deadline. Events are overtaking the premise. Soon I'll have to write an advice piece on how to escape a war zone.'

'I don't mean that. What will you tell Toby?'

'Nothing. None of it,' he said. 'None of what you shared.'

'I hate the word *shared*. I haven't shared anything. I've spoken up.' She looked directly at Mueller. 'Is he CIA?'

Mueller considered an easy lie, but he wasn't sure whom he wanted to protect – him or her. Or both. When their eyes met, he saw her judgment.

'I thought so,' she said. 'You aren't usually that slow to answer. I can read your hesitations. I can interpret silence.'

She looked at Mueller again. 'He didn't tell me what he did. I didn't ask. We had an interlude. That's all. The baggage of our lives was elsewhere – gone. We lived a pristine moment.' She clasped her hands, touching one finger, then another, eyes looking at nothing. A sad smiled adorned her face. She glowed. 'Everyone should have that feeling once in their life. To feel clean. In love. I will never forget it.'

She nodded. 'And apparently, he hasn't either. But you can't make the mistake of trying to reclaim what is gone. He has come here with his baggage and he is contaminating that memory.'

Liz opened the Land Rover's door and alighted to the driveway. Mueller found himself catching up with her as she strode to the house. Through the open front door there was a view into the courtyard where the little band of frustrated beachgoers relieved the heat with a swim in the pool. Cocktails were being served and food had been brought out. Jack held court, laughing, a boisterous big bull of a man clutching his double scotch on the rocks.

Liz suddenly stopped and turned to Mueller. 'Why did I marry Jack? That's what you must wonder. Well, I thought he would make a good father.'

Liz took Mueller's hand and led him to the ancient *algarrobo* tree that shaded the ground in a quiet spot beside the main house. Gnarled limbs hung off the thick muscular trunk and old roots were like veins in the earth. The canopy's shadow provided a hallowed peace from a hostile sun.

Liz stopped at an old, weathered marker set in the ground. Mueller calculated the boy's age from the two hundred-year-old dates. He looked at Liz, who had turned away and gazed at a new stone.

'There wasn't much to bury,' she said.

Mueller saw the name Clara carved into the fresh marble and there was a single date – the beginning and end of life.

'I was appalled at the thought that the little fetus would be incinerated as medical waste, so I gave her a name and we buried her. To remind me. Jack was supportive. I think the miscarriage was the only time in his life he wondered what I was going through.'

She contemplated the fresh flowers that had been placed around the marker. She waved off the hen pecking at the ground and shooed away a wandering pig. She knelt and slowly picked up small branches and leaves scattered by the storm. When she was done, she stood and looked down, lost in thought. At last she lifted her eyes to Mueller.

'I have found good in this. The purpose of my life – any life –

is to help other people get through their lives. If you know the comfortable life you enjoy is built on a foundation of misery deliberately imposed on a less fortunate people can you, in good conscience, do nothing, say nothing, remain silent? I can't. I haven't. People *can* change, you know.'

She stared hard at Mueller, almost contemptuously. She turned her back and walked into the house.

*

Dusk came and with evening the arrival of Toby Graham in a military jeep that had no markings. He strode right up to the front door, open wide for a cooling cross breeze, and stood like a statue watching the frivolity around the pool. Mueller looked up and saw him at the edge of the courtyard observing everything.

Much later, he recalled Graham's quiet demeanor, his hands at his side, and his face cast in the expression of a man reserving judgment, or making one.

'So, you didn't forget,' Jack greeted. 'We thought you'd stood us up.' He pointed with his half-smoked cigar. 'There's a seat for you and an empty glass. You missed the Papa Dobles.'

Graham approached with a quiet, pensive face and took the empty seat, nodding first in a courtly manner at the guests around the table, acknowledging Mueller, Jack, Katie, the Englishman, and then a quick glance at Liz.

Jack was at the head of the table and he poured himself a glass of imported red burgundy with the sloppy hand of a drinker who'd had his quota, and then he passed the bottle to Mueller, who passed it to Graham, who passed it along without pouring any for himself. The Clos de Tart passed to Liz and across to the Englishman, who noted the vintage and the producer, and nodded his approval. He poured himself a selfishly generous glass before passing it to Katie, who had paused in her story while the wine made its way around the table.

'Go ahead,' Liz said. 'What happened?'

'They wanted a photo of Castro.'

'Who wanted it?'

'*Time* magazine.' Her surprise silenced the table. 'They want something for their cover.' She had already given an account of trekking during the hurricane in search of her guide. Everyone had been hanging on to the details of the adventure when Graham arrived, and Jack, who'd grown restless and disapproving, had opened the wine.

'Yes, go ahead,' Jack said. 'Finish the story. Let's hear the rest of your lark.'

Katie looked around the table, taking in one face, then the next. Only Jack had slumped in his chair with ill-tempered skepticism. The others were entertained, and curious, and gazed at Katie. The story of her disappearance and return held everyone's attention and they were captive to the tale. The sedation of a big meal and alcohol made them fit only for placid listening. Dusk was falling and with it came the cobalt blue of arriving evening that left only flickering candlelight on Katie's face. She told her tale, occasionally referring to her notebook.

'We trekked in the rain on horseback, covered in plastic. There were two of us – a guide who met me and then handed me off to two rebels. We made it past a roadblock before daylight. The worst of the hurricane had hit, but the river was swollen. We had to detour upstream and cross at a narrows, which was still dangerous. The rushing water came up to the horses' necks and I lost one bag of film. We began our climb up the mountains on the other side. We trekked for six hours and the last part was thick forest, hardly a path at all, and the horses struggled on slick rocks.

'I didn't know we'd arrived at the rebel campsite until we were upon it and I saw we were in a clearing hidden under dense tree cover. There was an open-air shed with sheet-metal roof and two kerosene lamps. This was the field hospital and there was one young doctor who attended the wounded. There were four or five on cots from what I could see. It was crude and not particularly sanitary, but it looked orderly, well arranged, and there was mosquito netting over a table laid with surgical instruments. A gas burner boiled water. The hospital, I was told, had been erected two days earlier and it would be gone in a week so the air force would never spot it from the air.

'One plane did appear that afternoon. I could hear the engine approach and then it came low overhead just above the trees, but it didn't see us. A few minutes later we heard an explosion and a dense plume of smoke rose. They told me pilots dropped bombs on huts, or cattle, or randomly on the jungle. It was safer for a pilot to waste napalm bombs than to explain on his return to the airfield that he hadn't found a suitable target. You could see the jellied gasoline mushroom in thick black chemical smoke that left an acrid taste.

'The rebels laughed when they told me this. They have no respect for the air force or the army. They all had a story about some army platoon that surrendered its weapons when surrounded, shedding uniforms and taking an offered amnesty to go home.'

Katie looked around the table. The remains of dinner wilted in the evening humidity. Flickering orange light of the wicked candle gave the listening faces a warm glow.

'And this too,' Katie said suddenly, lifting her eyes from the notebook, 'surprised me. Fidel came the next morning. He'd been told I was there. He appeared like a hulking bear who wandered into the campsite. There were a dozen forest paths through the trees and he appeared from one of them – but not the one I expected. He just appeared. I looked up and saw him. He was unmistakable – the straggly beard, the cap, tall, wearing olive fatigues.

'He proudly carried an assault rifle and came with unsmiling bodyguards who protected him from me. They thought I might have a bomb in my bra.'

Katie presented her small chest in a comic pose as if to make a mockery of the thought she was capable of that offense. Jack grunted dyspeptically and the others laughed.

'They were polite when they searched me,' Katie continued. 'They had a woman pat me down and as she did she apologized in English, excusing their caution by telling me of all the attempts that had been made on Fidel's life. No one called him Castro or *comandante*. He was Fidel to all of them.'

Katie looked around the table. 'So, what is he like? That's the question you're asking yourselves.'

'Does he talk nonstop?' Callingwood asked. 'That's what they say about him. He can't stop talking. His speeches go on for hours. He drones on.'

'Godless communist,' Jack said lethargically, drawing on his cigar. 'Implacable ego. Surrounds himself with trigger-happy assassins.' Jack was animated with tobacco and alcohol and the full power of his impaired speech was on display. He turned to Graham. 'You've met him?'

Mueller looked at Graham, trying not to appear overly interested in how he might respond.

Graham looked around the table. He shrugged. 'There is no proof he is a – what did you call him? Godless communist? But it's convenient, certainly convenient for some in Washington, to make him out to be one to justify why we reject him.'

'Is that yes?'

'No. It's not yes. I haven't met him. I should like to. Wouldn't you?'

'Like to meet him?'

'Yes.'

Jack stared at Graham, contemplating the question. 'Sure. Why not? He sounds like a man you could talk to without fear of having your throat slit.'

'Go on, Katie,' Liz said. 'Tell us, for God's sake. Keep going. What is he like?' She shot a glance at her husband. 'If you're bored go to bed.' She looked at Katie. 'Now, you're going to be famous.'

Katie repeated the things she'd heard – the fables that surrounded the man. He was known to be unapproachable, a leader about whom little was known personally, and all communication to him passed through his secretary, Celia, a brisk woman, small and tough.

'Everyone suspects a romantic relationship, but I didn't see that at all. They are professional together, but there is the rumor. Of course, I wanted to get her photograph. Can you imagine the headline: "Fidel's Mistress?" But no one let me get close to that opportunity.'

'Other rumors?' she asked. 'They recruit teenage boys and arm them with scoped rifles. His brother resents Fidel's authority and the two have screaming arguments. He doesn't let on what his politics are, but the men around him who whisper in his ear are wedded to one ideology or another. He told me, and I have no reason to doubt him, that Americans will understand what he is trying to accomplish when they see the reforms he wants to carry out. He told me this with his big brown eyes open wide, his voice deepening, and I felt he was a hypnotist planting ideas that I'd take back. It was creepy. He is a persuasive speaker and he can be charming. He complimented my ad photos. How did he even know?'

Katie paused. 'I let him think he'd convinced me because it was in my interest to do so, and I let him go on. I was a patient listener and he has a big ego. The only thing he finds more interesting than to hear himself speak is to have others listen. I asked about the rumors. Why not? Had he memorized Dante's *Inferno* in prison? Did he never sleep twice in the same spot because he was afraid someone close would betray him? Had he spent his first honeymoon in the Plaza Hotel in New York? Did he have an illegitimate child in Mexico? He let me ask all the questions but he had nothing to say. He simply smiled. He enjoys letting himself be surrounded by mystery.'

Mueller leaned forward. 'Did he say anything personal?'

'He admires Mickey Mantle. They offered him five hundred dollars and a three-year contract. He said if he wasn't leading a revolution he'd be playing second base for the Yankees.'

Callingwood laughed hilariously, surprising the others, who looked at him.

Katie added, 'We didn't talk long. Men came with messages and interrupted us. There was a staccato rhythm to the brief conference as he sent or received messages, or radio transmissions came in. He sat beside me on his stump with an unlit cigar like a satisfied impresario. At one point, he got the news that five of his men had been killed in an ambush. His anger was volcanic and with that news the interview was over. He insisted I go and take close-ups of each body and that I should do that – his words – "so their martyrdom will not be forgotten by the world."'

'Did you get his photograph?' Liz asked.

'I did, yes, I did. At the beginning of the interview. I tried to get him holding the assault rifle. He was proud of it. Czech, he said, but he refused to be photographed with it.'

'Hide the negatives,' Jack huffed, extinguishing his cigar to save it. 'Fly to Miami. You're not safe here.'

Conversation ended and with it the evening was over, but no one moved for a long time. Jack sat apart from the rest in a sort of exile, an indistinct dark form at the end of the table, still like a contemplating Buddha. At last he stood and with wordless nod of good night made his way along the stone path. The Englishman also left, a prisoner of the curfew, and he struggled valiantly to improve the slack step of his drunken walk.

Mueller breathed deeply when Jack was gone and he felt the mood among the others relax as well. Jack was a big presence – a sun to their planets, hot when he wanted to be, and cold too. Mueller saw him a prisoner of his character who couldn't change, or wouldn't, Mueller didn't know which. Jack's departure created a void and quiet settled in among those who remained.

'Won't someone say something?' Katie snapped, looking around. 'I can't stand the silence. He's gone. Let's have a toast.'

Liz stood and turned to Graham. 'Your room is at the top of the stairs. There's a clean towel if you want to swim in the morning.'

Mueller detected a clipped politeness in her speech, as if she were addressing an unwanted visitor. She excused herself with a vague smile and followed the path Jack had taken to their bedroom. Mueller met Graham's expression, almost sullen, he thought. Mueller saw his weary nod, and watched him retreat into darkness. He'd come late, said little, and now he was off to his own guestroom.

Mueller found himself alone with Katie. They looked at each other across the table and Mueller raised his empty glass. 'Very clever,' he said. 'I'm impressed. Good work. I didn't expect it, but I'm not surprised.'

'You would have stopped me if I'd told you.'

'Probably, if I could, but I don't think I could. Stop you.' It crossed his mind that they were the last ones out and it would be an easy thing to pair up in her room, but he didn't allow himself that impulse. He suspected that she wouldn't accept the offer, and he didn't want to put himself out only to be rejected. They had found the limits of what they found interesting in each other.

She rose. Her eyes sparkled in silence. 'See you in the morning.'

He watched her glide away on her victory cloud – graceful, confident, self-assured. She'd gotten what she wanted. He knew their romance was over.

8

BOYHOOD

A FEW DAYS LATER, Mueller sat with his boots in the red dirt of a dry hill and glassed the small airfield with binoculars. He gripped the olive green metal and thumbed for focus. Sweat came through his shirt and darkened his back, and when the image sharpened he leaned forward. Bright midday sunlight gave a flat effect across the hundred yards where a DC-3 was parked by a small adobe terminal with limp windsock. Graham and two bearded Cubans unloaded a wooden crate from the plane. It took three men to receive it from a tanned blond man standing in the open cargo bay. The crate was the size of a coffin and it was placed on the tarmac. Nearby stood the Land Rover.

Mueller scanned the scene through the field glasses. The pilot had not shut down the engines and fierce wind from the cowling whipped their clothing. The fuselage markings were painted over, but Mueller knew this type of work at a remote airfield was a covert operation. Rifles strapped over the shoulders of the bearded men were U.S. Army M1 Garands with wood stock and stubby bullet clips.

He searched the spot. No cover. No, this spot wouldn't do for Pryce.

Again, he looked at the airplane. The sun was to his back so he knew they couldn't see him, but one of them pointed in Mueller's direction and he saw the bearded man direct Graham's attention to the hill. They hadn't seen him, but they'd seen something – light reflecting off the binoculars. Maybe his shadow.

Mueller stood. He waved. He made a descent from his perch where he left the field glasses on a flat rock.

'Hey there,' he shouted.

Graham had left the two men to finish their work, and he jogged to meet Mueller as he made his way down. They met halfway by the far end of the tarmac.

To the question that was obvious on Mueller's face, and the obvious mystery of the scene, Graham said, 'A little business, George. Embassy stuff. What's up?'

'Isn't that Jack's Land Rover?'

'Indeed it is. Liz lent it to me for the afternoon.' Graham paused. 'Jack's not holding a grudge. In a different time, a different place, different circumstances we'd be friends. He and I are alike.'

'Arrogant sonsofbitches.'

Graham laughed. 'He invited me – us – to lunch tomorrow. A little place in Nuevitas by the water. All of us.'

In that moment, Mueller had a choice of things to say – and there was a part of him that wanted to warn Graham that his little operation was putting his life at risk, but in the moment Mueller's stronger urge was to punish Graham for his treason

– or have him punished. Punish him too for his threat to Liz and Jack's marriage. He felt loyal to them. They'd had him to dinner, befriended him, looked after him, and tried to revive his romantic life.

'Let's talk,' Mueller said.

The flat tone of Mueller's voice got Graham's attention.

'Talk? About what? Are you concerned about me? Is that it?'

'It's part of the conversation that we haven't had.'

'Well, let's have it. But not here. Let's walk. Let the men finish their work. You're a man of mystery here and I don't need you to feed their suspicions.'

Graham led them a short way along the tarmac, then climbed the hill toward Mueller's perch.

'Up here,' Graham said. 'The view is superb.' He scampered up the rough red dirt terrain, dry now, baked by the sun. He got to the top and let his hand sweep across the breathtaking panorama – and it did in fact take Graham's breath away for an instant, a pause in his chest as his lungs caught up with his eyes. Mueller was surprised by Graham's reaction, because he assumed Graham had seen it before. The sea lay like a great sheet of rippled blue glass. Luminous breakers crumpled into shiny surf along the white sand beach. Above, a pale moon was opaque against the blue sky. Somewhere below from one of the adobe homes with walls topped by colorful glass shards pointing from cement – a sound. The bronchial voice of an old man, wheezing out a melancholy song.

Perhaps it was the view, or the view in combination with the singer, but Graham was transfixed. He stood silent for a long time.

'Every time I see this I feel the same thing.'

Graham pointed to the railroad tracks that snaked from the

port of Nuevitas inland and then disappeared behind dry hills.

'As a boy growing up on a farm in Ohio I'd hear a train pass through the rear of the property, and I always wished I was on it. Their whistles bewitched me. The call to travel. The need to leave home to find adventure in the world – and in my life, as it turns out, I've had my fill of it. You could say I've overdone it. But I did get away from that farm. Now when I think about those moments I don't think about myself standing there, a dreamy ten-year-old, but I think about my mother, my bedroom, the books on the shelves. The little boy with his life ahead of him. I miss all that. It's gone, of course, never to come back. Swallowed by time.'

Graham became quiet, pondering thoughts that he kept to himself. When he spoke again his voice was deep and resonant.

'Those books gave me a life I didn't have at home. I read all of them, devoured them, and they opened up my imagination. I was twelve when I read For Whom the Bell Tolls. Robert Jordan was a hero to me. I was fascinated by a young man who would fight and die for a cause in a country he hardly knew. He was cynical about the Republicans and distrustful of the Soviet allies, but I admired his courage and his sacrifice. Remember the final scene. The wounded Jordan chooses to die to save the poor Spanish souls he fought beside. Jordan's cause wasn't an ideology any longer, but a noble sacrifice for love. Remember what he said. The world is a fine place and worth fighting for and I hate very much to leave it. But he does, willingly. I got into this dirty business because of that book. The call to do good. Then I went to some dark places. I am part of this ugly world and I can diminish it further, or I can take a stand. You think it's strange, George, don't you? Me, thinking of myself as a good man. I see the skepticism in your face. I did my job. The work required me to do some bad things, some terrible things –'

Mueller waited for Graham to finish the thought, but the silence lengthened and Mueller was left to wonder what Graham held on to – regret, guilt, fear, darkness in his soul?

'Is that what you wanted to hear from me?' Graham suddenly asked. 'Is that what they want to hear in Headquarters? Do they care?' Graham let his eyes drift from the view and he settled on Mueller. 'We all walk with our devils.'

Graham nodded at the DC-3. 'We all have a job to do. It's leaving soon.'

'Will you be on it?' Mueller asked.

Graham turned slowly to face Mueller, pondering. 'Should I be?'

'I would if I were you.'

'George, you can't say that and not say what's on your mind. What do you know?'

'Frank Pryce is in Camaguey. He thinks you're at risk.'

'He doesn't care about me. I'm trouble for him. He's a sonofabitch. Add him to your list.'

'He thinks you'll be picked up. Or worse. Alonzo's thugs are looking for you.' Mueller pointed at the two men unloading the airplane. 'Do you trust them?'

'I don't trust anyone. I got out of Budapest. I slipped onto a ship in Algeria. I expect to get out of here. I'm not the romantic who wants to die on this bleeding piece of earth.'

'Then leave now.'

'I have business to finish. More planes are coming in. Now is not the time to leave. But when I do go I won't be alone.'

Graham turned and began a slow descent from the hill to the airfield. He had gone a few yards when he turned and shouted to Mueller, who had not stirred. 'I love her, you know. And she loves me.'

Graham continued down, heels digging into the earth to slow his descent until he knew that Mueller had gained on him and he stopped. He let Mueller catch up.

He looked at Mueller. 'Jack knows about Liz and me. She told him. He wants to be mature about all this.'

*

It was always the quiet of night that stilled the fever of the day. Mueller lay in his room in Hotel Colon and read over the notes he'd made for his report to the director that he would file when hurricane-damaged communications to the U.S. were restored. He was careful to separate what he knew about the man, and what he knew about the case officer. As he read the entries he realized that without any active intention he was building a case against Graham. He had crossed the line from biographer to investigator without knowing it. The man he'd uncovered was a dark shadow reflected in a hall of mirrors – vaguely like the man he remembered. He pondered Graham. He was curious about the hard puzzle that was Graham's mind.

Mueller's notes in his diary from that day had stopped there.

9

ALL THIS

ALL THIS WAS THE phrase Mueller kept in the back of his mind when he stood among the group assembled at the waiting vehicles in Hacienda Madrigal's driveway. Jack was in his Land Rover with Katie and a sullen Liz, and he honked impatiently at Graham and the Englishman, who chatted by the pickup.

They were all together again, Mueller thought, all of them plus Callingwood, who'd showed up with the terrible excuse that he had the afternoon free, and no one was rude enough to reject his request to join lunch at a roadside restaurant that served fish caught only hours before. It was the promise of adventure that lured them from the confinement of the ranch.

'Here,' Jack said. He threw the keys to the pickup at Mueller. 'Give them to Graham. He says he knows the place. He can take Callingwood. Tell him to stay close. We're not stopping for anything. Keep going if you see trouble.'

The little party was using the charm of a fisherman's shack to escape the oppression of the war. They all wanted to embrace the trip as a way to lighten the day, contain their drama, and preserve decorum, but Mueller felt jeopardy in the fragile peace. Pleasant conversation and careless laughter carried on and found expression in the absurd scene of gimpy Maximo chasing the three legged dog chasing a squawking hen. All the laughter. All the false unconcern. Mueller felt all this during the thirty-minute drive to Nuevitas. He listened to Jack and Katie dispute some nonsense that Mueller did not remember, except to remember that it was hotly said.

*

The argument began in the usual way, from a surprise that shouldn't have been a surprise that came in the midst of an otherwise pleasant conversation. Jack was driving fast along the flat coast road when Mueller asked a question that he thought was innocent enough, but he'd unknowingly touched a nerve.

Jack stared. 'I'm not sure what business it is of yours how I chose to spend my time, but I'll tell you. No, that's not why I flew to Havana. I happened to be seeing that man Pryce on other business, and he had done me the favor of buying that book. He has his contacts in the Mafia. They trade in all sorts of stuff. I'd told him to keep an eye out, and he knew a family in Vedado liquidating their assets to move to Miami.'

Jack pointed to an old leather-bound volume. 'The 1889 edition of The Coffee Plantation. I've wanted it for some time. So, Pryce arranged to get it for me through his contacts, but as I said, I wasn't there for that. He happened to have found it, which I was happy about, but I'd gone to see him about another matter. He gave me the rundown on Graham.'

Jack turned to Liz, who gazed out the window. She seemed to know she'd been drawn into the conversation and she met Jack's gaze.

'Yes,' Liz said. She whispered her answer quickly and economically.

'I asked Pryce about him. Pryce has his ways of getting information. He wrote something up.'

Mueller found himself staring at Jack. He felt the sly hand of Pryce's chicanery at work.

'He owed me a favor!' Jack protested. 'Why not a little dirt on our mysterious new friend, Toby Graham? He's not my friend, but he's your friend.'

Jack handed a file to Mueller. 'Take a look.'

Mueller removed a typed report from a large manila envelope and he saw how the typist's heavy hand on the *s* key had struck through the paper. As was his habit, he took in the scope of the document before he read – no date, nothing to reveal its provenance, only a cryptic heading – re: Toby Graham.

Mueller scanned to the end and then read the first paragraph.

'Read it out loud,' Jack said. 'I think we're all curious.'

Mueller looked at Liz.

'Go ahead.'

'It says here that he was inserted into Naples in 1944 working for the OSS in advance of the Allied invasion. Apparently, he kept a diary of his work, which was a violation of every rule of caution because it put him and his colleagues, the entire operation, at risk if it fell into the hands of the Nazis. It says that he was reckless.'

'There's more,' Jack said.

'Yes, there's quite a bit more. It says he was well liked, self-confident, undaunted, presumptuous, impudent, bold, cocksure.' Mueller looked up. 'Sounds like him.'

'Go ahead, finish,' Jack said.

Mueller paraphrased. 'He operated behind enemy lines, putting his life at risk, and he did so courageously.' Mueller looked up from the page. 'I'm sure he had fear too. A man who puts his life at risk is afraid, and if he says he isn't, he's a liar. To be brave, really brave, a man has to be terrified.'

'You're making that up,' Jack snapped. 'That's not what it says.'

'I added what I know.'

'Read it. Or I'll read it.'

'This report cites another report.' Mueller read, starting again at the beginning. '"He landed on a hostile coast and got to Naples with no one there in advance to hide him. He displayed courage in the face of the enemy. He lived for months as an impostor using his wits and knowledge of Italian to gather intelligence, and he did that even as his local agents were caught, tortured, executed. In return, he tracked down and assassinated the head of the local Gestapo. And he killed two men with his bare hands. He had something beyond courage – foolhardiness, bravado. An appetite for danger. You know the type of man – a taste for danger that is sweeter than a shot of whiskey. And with it,"' Mueller stopped and he looked at Jack.

'Go ahead.'

Mueller added, 'Well that's what the original report said, and now we get to Pryce's judgment.' He read. '"Graham thought top-level OSS officers in Allied Headquarters incompetent and confused about the state of the German defenses. He ignored instructions delivered to him by coded radio transmitter because he disagreed with the orders, and he conducted his own operations that he believed better disrupted German defenses. He called his superiors amateurs in his rants in his radio transmissions. In the final months of the siege Allied Headquarters ignored Graham and stopped sending him spare parts for his radio. Before Naples fell, the colonel in Headquarters who supervised Graham was transferred out of the command when the first Allied assaults failed miserably. Graham was right. Entries that described his disobedience were expunged from his record."'

Jack spoke up. 'He was reprimanded. Read the end. He was dressed down, then forgiven. Right, George. You've skipped a paragraph. He was called immature. Arrogant. After the war, he was drummed out of the OSS because he hadn't toed the line and in the military it matters if you win the war, but it matters more if you disobey. No one forgets someone who disregards orders, and he paid the price.'

'What's he doing in Cuba?' This from Katie.

Jack turned to Mueller. 'You must know.'

Mueller smiled tolerantly. 'Where did you get this information?'

'You don't believe it?'

'That's not my question. Let's say it's true, and I'm willing to believe it is, I'm curious how Pryce got hold of it – and why he gave it to you.'

'I said I asked for it. That's why. A man shows up in your home. Takes an interest in your wife. Wouldn't you be curious who he is?'

Jack added a few other things about Graham he'd picked up from men who worked on the ranch and dealt with squatters. Mueller assumed they were the embellishments of ranch hands eager to give a false account to please Jack. Mueller had heard some of the talk, but he knew Graham well enough to discern the exaggerations that attached themselves to a fact and slowly, but inevitably, the original truth took on a distorted life. People repeated scandalous stories because the malicious untruths made for good gossip, and when the stories were about a person you didn't care for, or others had a grudge against, it was the gossip that you preferred to hear.

'He's out there being a do-gooder,' Jack said. 'He says he's making a difference here, giving away sacks of rice from his jeep. Handing out cigarettes to kids. It's all show. An act.' Jack looked at Liz. 'You've fallen for it.'

'Fallen for what?'

'He's trying to impress you with the alms he hands out. You think a man like Toby Graham has a good bone in his body?'

Liz stared. 'You are a horrible cynic, aren't you? No good deed goes unquestioned, does it? You insult people to feel better about yourself. He wouldn't go around your back to dig up dirt on you. He has manners.'

'Manners?' Jack glared. 'Is that what you call his interest in you? Tracking you down. Renting a house in Vedado that looks into your bedroom.'

Liz blanched. Her lips parted slightly, then closed. She looked off at the flat ribbon of highway, then suddenly she faced Jack. Her lips quivered and her whole body seemed to tremble in a way she sought to control. She spoke in a whispery voice. 'Who are you to judge me?'

Mueller knew she'd always been able to put on a brave front, but she'd gone cold. She didn't seem to care anymore – to care about her charade. Something liberated her, freed her, from the pattern of accommodating Jack. Husband and wife sat a few feet apart, but the distance between them had widened to a gulf.

Jack looked at Mueller. 'She won't leave me. Where is she going to go?'

No one spoke. Mueller felt the profound quiet among them, and everyone was struck dumb. Mueller heard the question repeat in his mind – *Where is she going to go?* – and Mueller felt the terrible weight of an answer. Mueller felt displaced in time as they sped along to the promised seaside luncheon, and he worried about what lay ahead.

Mueller found distraction in the passing landscape, the *guajiros* in oxcarts, or cane cutters working fields. He saw too a young woman who stood at the concrete kilometer marker, alone, with a leather-handled suitcase. Her parasol was protection against the molten sun. She suddenly stood and waved down the speeding Land Rover. Mueller was startled to see her come right toward the vehicle, and then the Land Rover swerved and sped past. Jack had avoided her, pulling into the left lane and then glancing in the rearview mirror.

The woman waved energetically. It was an urgent, astonished wave – the wave of a startled acquaintance.

Mueller saw her as the Land Rover sped by, and then he looked back to make certain. It was Jack's girl. Mueller hadn't recognized her at first. The scarf, a long, loose pleated dress, and her sandals were nothing like the high heels she wore onstage. Mueller saw her step into the middle of the road and stare at the caravan as it sped away.

*

The answer to Jack's question came two hours later at the seaside restaurant. Mueller heard Jack's elaborate compliment of the outdoor restaurant, and he'd gotten over his surprise that it was just two wood tables, a few chairs, and a shack with an outdoor kitchen. A thatched umbrella covered the dirt floor and beyond the shade, an open pit of embers still burned fat off a spitted pig. Chickens scraped the ground and nearby hogs ate from a pile of kitchen scraps. The view of the pounding surf was magnificent, as promised, and the food was good, or at least fresh, and they sat with a breeze that kept mosquitoes away. Roast pig and fish had been served by the fisherman's wife, a heavy, toothless woman with muscular hands that poured small portions of a rum from unlabeled bottles. Lunch had been pleasant, quiet, broken by news of the war, and a few concerns about Katie's flight, which had been canceled, so her effort to leave was thwarted and she kept herself busy staying away from public view in Camaguey. Graham offered to get her out on one of the DC-3s.

Mueller saw all this with his observer's eye and thought how well things were getting along. Surprisingly well. They had the lightheartedness of people willing themselves to have a good time. He felt it. Catalogued it.

'What new topic should we pick to enliven things?' Katie said. 'Everyone's so down. We came out here to get away from the gloom.' Katie looked at Liz and then at the others, who picked at the food. The crisped head of the roast pig was a centerpiece on the table. 'Gloom, gloom, gloom. Sun in the sky, clouds on your faces.'

'You're leaving soon,' Liz said. 'We'll still be here waiting for the end to come.'

'Let's dance,' Katie said. 'There's a guitar.' She looked at Mueller. 'Will you dance?'

He waved her off. 'Two left feet.'

Katie stood and performed a two-step *cha-cha-cha* for the

group, first flirting with Callingwood, who seemed astonished by the invitation, and then she dragged Liz from her chair. She protested, and resisted, but finally allowed herself to be led to the clear area and reluctantly made a few dance steps, but she gave in to the Latin rhythms when the fisherman's wife took up the guitar and strummed a song, singing with a magnificent voice. The fisherman joined in with a percussive up-tempo beat on the maracas, making whooping calls. Katie led Liz through orchestrated steps and suddenly the music stopped and they were beside themselves, giddy with embarrassment. They danced a mambo, following the makeshift band, and then another and another.

'You've stopped,' Katie said to Liz.

'My legs are tired. It's hot.' She sank in her chair and drank from a coconut husk that sprouted a straw topped with a tiny Cuban flag.

It was then that Mueller saw discord raise its quarrelsome head.

Jack had angled his legs straight out and shifted his eyes from the pig head. Jack fixed his gaze on Graham. From time to time Jack looked away, or added rum to his empty glass, or moved his bulk in a contorted way, but each time he came back and his eyes settled on Graham.

'Toby,' Jack said, raising his voice, to draw attention. 'I understand you were a war hero.' Jack's sarcastic tone drew everyone's attention. 'You earned a medal for some dangerous shenanigans.'

'Medal?' Graham said. 'Dangerous shenanigans? Everyone in the war took risks. I got a medal. Others didn't. Luck of the draw.'

'You got a medal and then they took it away from you. What

211

do you call that? Unluck of the draw? Or maybe it's called insubordination. You were shit-canned.'

Jack's agitation deepened and his voice had risen to an insulting vibrato. The worst in Jack emerged with alcohol and Mueller had counted four rum and Cokes when Jack made his remark. All pretense of a fun afternoon over a pleasant meal was gone.

'I wasn't shit-canned,' Graham said. 'I was relieved of my duties by an incompetent captain who later was removed from his command when it became clear he was wrong.'

'You think you can come here – like you did in Naples – and bully your way around. Thinking you have permission. That's your style, I see.'

Mueller put a restraining hand on Jack's shoulder.

'Stay out of this, George,' Jack said. To Graham, 'I think you're a moocher who has taken advantage of our hospitality. Pretending to be one kind of man when you're actually another – a liar, a conniver, a house guest who covets my wife.'

Appalled silence fell like a curtain on the small group.

'I think you should leave,' Jack said. 'Don't show up again at our place.'

Graham leaned forward to shorten the distance to Jack. He leveled his eyes and looked to speak, but didn't.

'Did you hear me?'

Graham nodded. His whole body rose slightly and he spoke defiantly. 'Liz is unhappy. Your marriage is over.' Graham took Liz's hand protectively to soften the suddenness of his declaration. 'Liz and I will be leaving together.'

Liz withdrew her hand. She stood and turned away from both men, horrified.

'Sit,' Jack commanded. 'What's this all about? Liz unhappy?' He almost laughed.

'Liz is fed up with you,' Graham said. 'You haven't been good to her. You're a scoundrel.'

'Toby,' Liz snapped.

'No,' Jack said, 'I want to hear this.'

'She doesn't want to stay with you. It's that simple. You don't see it, do you?'

Jack didn't take his eyes off Graham, and he pulled his body up from its slump, rising like a man thrown off a horse. 'Who are you to tell me my wife is leaving me? Here at this table. You think Liz is done with our marriage? Is that right? You think that somehow, in an imaginary world of your own, that she wants you? Well, she hardly knows you. And I doubt she knows your work.'

Graham spoke calmly. 'Liz can speak for herself.'

'Liz. Well?'

Everyone turned to Liz and an unwanted spotlight fell on her. She turned away from the view of the beach. A black fly alighted on the Cuban flag sprouting from her cocktail. Its hint of celebration mocked her startled expression and she continued to stare at the fly, hoping for rescue.

She looked up. 'I wish you wouldn't ask that question. Not here. Not now. Not among all of us.' Her eyes darted among the faces at the table. She stared at Jack. 'We don't have to have this conversation now. I'm sorry you've brought it up again. You've spoiled the afternoon, haven't you!'

Jack looked at Graham. 'We were doing okay before you showed up. You were wrong to come here. A stranger, showing up uninvited.'

'I'm not a stranger to Liz.'

Mueller saw Jack's lip curl and Mueller again put his hand on Jack's shoulder.

Jack stared at Graham. 'Who are you to judge us?' He paused.

'She gave you a couple of days of her life and took some pleasure from you. That doesn't give you a claim on our life. And it doesn't mean that she's leaving me.'

Liz groaned. She put her hands over her ears and when she looked again at Jack her eyes had reddened. 'Stop,' she said. 'Stop,' she shouted. 'Stop it. This day is ruined. You've ruined it.'

Liz had a look of pity on her face. She calmed and looked at Jack. She spoke through red eyes in a measured voice. 'You let the garden of our marriage go to seed. There were flowers we planted to remind us who we used to be, but they've withered. Dried up here in this place. All our sunshine days of memory are not enough to let us ignore the weeds. It's over. It's been over a long time. I'm sorry, Jack. I can't do this anymore.'

Liz allowed Graham to take her hand, but then she pushed it away. Liz stood. She looked at Mueller. 'Will you come with me? Drive with me home?' She looked at Jack with furious pity. 'The keys, please.'

She walked alone toward the Land Rover. Katie ran after her. They escaped from the feeling of catastrophe that remained at the table. The six of them had come in two vehicles and the group had to divide themselves for the return, and there came a moment when the loyalty to husband and wife was to be tested.

Callingwood was the last to choose, and by the time he did, the other three had already divided up. Liz got in the driver's seat of the Land Rover. She looked back at Graham, who stood at one table. 'Will you come with us?'

Katie took the passenger seat. Graham removed Liz from behind the wheel and relieved her from the responsibility to navigate home in the dark in her heightened state.

Mueller saw how Liz's invitation to Graham confirmed

the answer to the question Jack had posed. Her choice of companion for the ride home was a declaration. Mueller didn't want to leave Jack by himself. Mueller had a sense of loyalty and he also felt that it would be unwise to abandon Jack.

'Don't stick around for me,' Jack said. 'I don't need my hand held. Go ahead, George, join them. I see you want to. Go ahead. I won't be alone. I've got him for company.' He nodded carelessly at Callingwood.

Mueller joined the others in the Land Rover. He looked back. Jack was alone with an Englishman he didn't like. Mueller saw a lonely figure, but not a defeated man. A proud and confused man.

10

ACCIDENT

MUELLER SAT BESIDE LIZ in the rear of the Land Rover. The backseat had been lowered flat to accommodate the wood crate, and Mueller and Liz sat on it, making it as comfortable as they could. The Land Rover bounced on the rough road and Mueller found Liz thrown into his lap when the vehicle swerved to avoid a rut.

Mueller saw Graham hunched forward on the steering wheel, eyes trying to make out the perils. Headlights tunneled the darkness and narrowed their world to the arc of the headlamps.

He found himself wanting to tell Graham to slow down, but each time the Land Rover swerved and the impulse to caution Graham rose in him, the Land Rover slowed, and Mueller thought it unnecessary to speak. Mueller didn't want to challenge Graham. There was an ominous mood in the car that stilled them, quieted them. A declaration had been made. A line crossed. It weighed heavily. No one spoke. Mueller succumbed to fatigue. He didn't have the will, or desire, to ask Graham to be cautious. Mueller felt Liz beside him and he tried to imagine her devastation.

*

Mueller was asleep when the accident happened. He got the details of the death later from Katie, who had been awake at the moment the Land Rover took the sharp curve by the river and struck the woman.

Graham had been going fast when he entered the curve. Headlights illuminated the road, but beyond the light it was hard to discern the shapes that appeared and receded with hypnotic rhythm. Coming through the sharp turn the road divided. One fork led to the airport and the other went over the bridge, and it was there that the woman leapt from the culvert. She put herself in the path of the Land Rover, Katie said. She had waved her arm and run into the road like a ghost, her face paled by the bright headlights. She seemed to want the car to stop. 'She waved her arms at us. Waved and waved.' But Katie admitted this conclusion only came to her afterward. In the moment, her appearance on the road was unexpected, sudden, frightening, and her first thought was of rebels.

'I felt the brakes lock. There was a skid and then I heard a terrible cry that was cut short when we struck her. It was a horrible scream,' Katie said. 'A terrible cry.'

*

Mueller stood over the body. The young woman lay by the roadside culvert where she'd been thrown. One leg was twisted under her back, her arms were flung to either side, frozen in death. Her face was ashen, eyes wide and unfocused, and there was a scarlet stream on her neck flowing from a wet spot in her dark hair. Her head scarf was bloodied. Her broken parasol lay at her side.

Mueller recognized her, but it took a moment for him to remember her name – and not think of her, as he always had, as Jack's girl. That shorthand didn't adequately describe the young woman. It felt wrong to see her whole being through the narrow lens of her scandalous association.

'Ofelia,' he said. 'That's her name.'

'I will come back for her,' Graham said. 'I'll drop everyone at the house and I'll return for her.'

No one objected to his suggestion. He made it confidently and the paralysis of shock made it easy to acquiesce in his decision.

Later, when they were at Hacienda Madrigal, Mueller wondered about the suggestion. Mueller had accompanied Liz and Katie inside, and when he was confident they were settled, he returned to the driveway. The Land Rover pulled up, Graham at the wheel, and Mueller knew he'd driven back to the scene of the accident, as he said he would.

Mueller opened the rear door to retrieve Liz's shawl, and it was then that he saw the wood crate was gone. Mueller stared at Graham, trying not to judge the man – for certainly the death was an accident – but Graham had had the presence of mind and calculating intelligence to hide the thing that would compromise him.

The two men faced each other. Graham brushed dust from his dirtied hands and wiped clotted mud from his boot. When he spoke his voice had no distress, no regret, no hint of the evening's catastrophe. He had the calm bearing of a man accustomed to turning unexpected jeopardy to a manageable outcome.

'There was a suitcase roadside. She'd packed her things for a long trip.' He paused. 'She came out of nowhere. There was no way to stop.'

'Where is she?'

'I told the police there was a body by the side of the road. Hit and run. Filed a report. They wanted the details. No, I didn't say it was us. I didn't want to get Jack in trouble. He doesn't need to answer questions about this. It was an accident. She's dead. We don't need to complicate things.' His irritation showed.

One hour later, Mueller sat on the verandah after the household settled for the evening. When Jack arrived he was given the news, but no one gave him the name – he seemed to guess. Everyone left unsaid most of what they knew, and they went about their evening in stunned, shocked quiet.

Mueller pondered the easy way Graham sloughed responsibility for the accident and dressed himself in the suit of a righteous protector. Graham's odd summary and misleading comments were the product of a mind schooled by years of self-preservation. *How's Liz taking it?* Graham had asked. Mueller remembered the question because it seemed to come from a genuine place. Mueller thought about the question as he sat on the verandah, and he began to make connections. He came to understand Graham a little better. He came to see how Toby Graham carried the terrible burden of a man at war with himself.

Shortly before midnight Mueller rose and made his way inside, but passing the living room he saw a light on and he entered thinking that Graham was up. He saw no one at first.

Sleeplessness and stress distorted and magnified the room. The marble fireplace had a cold monumental whiteness and the grand piano's gleaming black surface mirrored the chandelier. Tall windows were obsidian columns looking out to the night. His most vivid memory of the room was looking about and *not* seeing Graham at the fireplace – so still he was invisible.

Thinking he was alone, Mueller moved to the window and in the distance, he saw the headlights of a far-off vehicle headed to the hacienda. He gazed at the speeding vehicle illuminated by moonlight, which laid a false peace on the landscape. It was long past curfew.

'Police, I suspect.'

Startled, Mueller turned around. He saw Graham had pulled away from the wall like a painting come to life.

'You suspect?'

'They'll probably want to talk with me.'

'You gave a report.'

Graham grunted. 'A clerk. They might have more questions. I suspect they will.' Graham raised an eyebrow. 'There's too much to risk. I have to leave.'

Mueller stepped up to Graham, jaw set, eyes narrow. The two men stood close. Mueller embraced Graham, startling him, but then Graham too raised his arms and the two men felt the bond of their long, troubled acquaintance. Two old schoolmates found in the affectionate moment a measure of calm. They held each other, but were separated by a peril. Silence clamored. Graham pulled away.

'Stay in my hotel room. They won't look there.'

Graham almost laughed. 'They'll look there, of course. And I suppose I shouldn't be suspicious that you would suggest an unsafe place thinking it would be safe. Best you not know what's next. I only need one thing from you, George. One small favor. When I'm ready to go I need you to bring Liz to me. Will you do that?'

A chastened Mueller looked at Graham. 'Of course.'

'I will be gone for a few days.'

Mueller didn't believe that Graham would leave Cuba for good on his own. Graham's eyes were fiery, the eyes of an idealist. He wouldn't give up. He might leave, but he'd be back. The front door of life had burst open and Graham's fortune had blown in. Mueller stood on the hacienda's porch and watched Graham disappear into the night, ahead of the approaching vehicle. His jeep stirred dust as it sped off and the moving cloud stained the empty plain. Everything began to end that night.

11

INVESTIGATION

THE CONDUCT OF JUSTICE carried on in predictable ways in the ensuing week. Rebel movements and ongoing skirmishes in the province didn't diminish the diligence of the local police detective, but his work was slowed by the increasing petty crime that accompanied anxiety about the war. The detective carried on by himself in a plodding and dedicated way, believing that civil strife was no excuse to abandon law and order. Then he got the unexpected support of SIM, and he was happy about that. Captain Alonzo showed up when the news of the death, and the circumstances, got wider attention. The investigation picked up. A witness came forward with a statement that he'd seen a Land Rover on the road late, and he'd noted the time, 9:30 p.m., because it was past curfew. The Land Rover was the only vehicle out at that hour. That's what the police detective said when he interviewed Jack.

The witness, a squatter, had a shack off the main road. He'd been checking his chickens against the rats that preyed on the chicks when he saw the Land Rover speed by. Then later the witness admitted he'd seen a pickup truck pass on the same stretch of road.

Few things are absolutely clear in the aftermath of an accident at night, and Mueller knew it would take time for the dedicated detective to assemble the partial and often contradictory statements into a plausible narrative, and then, within the limits of the available evidence, establish that a crime had been committed. And in the process, he also had to discern which of the contradictory statements were lies, which poor memories, and which honest errors in a confusing situation.

*

Mueller's conversation with Liz took place in the morning a day later. She approached him as he was finishing breakfast in the Hotel Colon. He was alone in the small dining room enjoying coffee. The hotel was closing. Most of the guests had already left for Havana, if they could hire a car, or a private airplane, or managed to find a spot in the bus organized by the embassy. The place felt deserted, but the service had improved as he was now the only guest. Two waiters stood at the ready when Liz sat opposite Mueller. They were instantly at her side offering coffee. She had come for him and his bags. He would be moving into the house until he found a way to reach Havana.

Liz sat. She removed her sunglasses. The morning heat added a rosy blush to her cheeks.

'I'm leaving Jack,' she said.

Mueller waited for her to elaborate.

'I'm not asking for your approval. I don't need to have that, but I am asking for your understanding. I think of that woman – that poor dead girl. She jumped out because she thought Jack was driving.' She stiffened. 'He begrudged me my moment of weakness and he was still going to set up that girl in Miami.'

Her eyes were furious. 'I can't forgive him. He poisoned the earth of our marriage.'

'You think Toby is a better man?'

'He's better toward me.' She contemplated Mueller and added in a low voice, 'A man can change. You don't know the Toby I know.'

'But do you know him?' he snapped.

She was startled by Mueller's sharp tone. 'Are you jealous? Is that what this is about?'

Mueller hadn't expected to hear that from her. Their brief romance had been early in her engagement to Jack. She had begun to complain about Jack's restlessness, but had not yet begun to openly suffer. The infidelity had come at the end of a boisterous New Year's Eve party in Vienna. Warm laughter had turned to silliness and then came a startling kiss and the passion culminated in rushed, awkward sex in the bathroom. He had been open to continuing the relationship, but Liz excused the incident as a friendly mistake before marriage. But for Mueller the friendly mistake was a durable memory.

'Toby is a good man,' Mueller said, 'but he is a dangerous man. He has a good heart. A lonely heart. He lives under a dark shadow.'

'I know the shadow.' She looked at Mueller. 'Who are you to judge him?'

Mueller was certain the direction of their conversation would only further divide them, and he wanted to respect their history. He suspected she'd already made up her mind. 'How can I help?'

'They've come by looking for him. I said to speak with you. Tell them I was driving. Would you do that? It will come out better if things don't point to him.' She paused. 'When his plane arrives, I am leaving with him.'

And in that moment Mueller suddenly understood that Liz knew what was in the wood crate. He looked at her and the innocence he'd seen was strangled. Everyone can change, he thought. The sight of dead boys hanging from lampposts can change you. It had changed her. She had become Graham's accomplice. He saw that in her pleading eyes.

12

FUNERAL

MUELLER WAS SEATED IN the rear of the cathedral on the side aisle, but he was conscious nevertheless of drawing attention. He was with Katie and Liz and they were the only Americans among the large, restless crowd gathered solemnly at Ofelia Betancourt's funeral. Knowing the deceased, many of those seated in the packed church knew each other, and among them the death of a young woman of great beauty, whose life was abruptly cut short, struck a chord. Grief was abundant among the mourners and fierce sorrow was worn proudly among a contingent near the nave who appropriated her death for their own outrage. The uncertain circumstances of her death, its having come at night on the road, and the shocking prematureness of it, even in a time of war, contributed to the atmosphere of apprehension.

Incense hung heavy in the cathedral and was a cloud over the overflowing crowd which came to witness the farewell mass.

Black clothing was everywhere and women, even young girls, had lace scarves and veils. Only the contingent of young men near the front wore fatigues. This clutch of men seemed to have come straight from the mountains. Their boots had red earth, and their faces had straggly beards and the likeness of rebels. Police were nowhere to be seen inside the cathedral.

Liz had come at Mueller's urging to pay her respects and to atone for whatever fault she bore as a complicit witness. Katie came to observe. To be a camera, not to hold one. Mueller was compelled to attend by the same ambiguous feelings, and then Graham sent word that he would use the funeral as a pretense to collect Liz. So their little group was formed.

They were seated in the back and as Mueller waited for the service to begin he happened to glance at the cathedral's doors. It was then he saw Frank Pryce, silhouetted, who acknowledged Mueller with a simple nod, and then Mueller looked around to see if there were police, but there were none, or none in uniform. Only Frank Pryce. He watched from a distance and ignored the crowd. The trap was baited. Mueller looked at Liz and in the corner of his eye he picked out the arched door to the cloisters where Graham said he would wait.

Mueller was mystified by the rituals of the Catholic mass, but he saw how the mystery seemed to comfort the mourners. It wasn't a memorial service. No one eulogized the dead girl, who lay in an open coffin in quiet repose in a white dress. Mueller looked at her, as did everyone, struck by her beauty. Liz had bowed her head and only she did not look. There was no mention of how she died. Nor was there mention of her rebelliousness, or her scandal. Mueller assumed that most of the mourners knew what he knew, or some version of it, and he suspected many among them were thinking of an unforgiving God. Liz too prayed.

A long, mournful chime from the cathedral's bell punctuated the silence and signaled the end of the mass. Six men, who sat near the nave, most likely male relatives, given their prominent position, lifted the casket. A spontaneous chorus of 'Mama son de la loma' rose from the rebel contingent that walked behind the somber pallbearers.

Mueller watched Betancourt come up the aisle behind his dead sister – a young man in black with an old man's vacant eyes. He looked straight ahead to the sunlight pouring in through the cathedral's doors.

Mueller observed him in his grief and in one unexpected moment he saw Betancourt's face turn, a slow conscious shift of a few degrees, and their eyes met. It was a brief encounter, hardly a second, but Mueller did not mistake the look on his face – angry grief, vengeful grief.

Mueller, Katie, and Liz were in the middle of the crowd leaving the cathedral, and they were hidden among the many mourners making their way to the doors. Frank Pryce moved toward them, against the crowd, and he pulled Mueller to one side and spoke confidentially. Words were exchanged. Mueller nodded into the church at the arched door.

'Who chose the spot?' Pryce asked.

'He did. He has the advantage.'

'I don't think so.'

'Then you don't know him,' Mueller snapped. He pointed to Pryce's linen jacket. 'What's the gun for?'

'In case something happens.'

'Something will happen. Where's Ruden?'

Mueller didn't get an answer from Pryce, and the rebuff was the first thing that irritated Mueller. He rejoined Katie and Liz, whose quizzical expressions he ignored, and he pointed toward the exit. They were among the last to leave the cathedral and they joined other stragglers who congregated on the wide stone steps. The rebel contingent had already reached the plaza and they fired guns into the air to release defiant grief. Mueller had put on his sunglasses against the glare to look at the commotion. It was then that he saw two green Oldsmobile sedans parked across the street. One driver in his tan SIM uniform was being taunted by the crowd.

Mueller pondered the unlikely presence of the Oldsmobiles and suddenly a hard knot formed in his gut. He looked back at Pryce, but sunlight made the inside of the church impenetrable, and then, again, he stared at the two cars. Only one driver. The scale of the treachery struck Mueller all at once. Accumulating evidence pointed inexorably to betrayal. Pryce's silence. The presence of the Servicio de Inteligencia Militar. The absent second driver.

Mueller turned to the two women. 'Go to the Land Rover. I will meet you there. Wait ten minutes. No longer. If I don't show up, go straight to the house.'

Mueller entered the empty cathedral and ran toward the arched door, his footsteps echoing in the holy space. Through the door he came upon a private garden surrounded by a covered walkway. The quadrangle of green was a well-tended medieval garden that sat inside the cloisters' colonnade. Mueller looked past the flower beds and beyond the shaded columns, eyes alert. He heard urgent voices somewhere and rapid footsteps. A young boy no older than ten, in a long coarse cotton robe, emerged from behind one column, where he'd been hiding. He pointed to stone steps at one end of the cloisters that rose to the square Moorish-tiled bell tower.

Mueller took the stairs two at a time. Sweat formed on his

brow and his lungs took in gulping breaths as he dashed up stone stairs that wrapped around the center well. He climbed one landing to the next, making his way up five flights, raising his eyes toward the huge bronze bell that dominated the belfry. Camaguey's red-tile rooftops came into view on his way up, and a hot wind whistled through each open floor. The bell's hemp rope dropped through the well to the ground floor.

Footsteps he'd heard when he started up were silent and now he heard voices. Two men, Graham and Pryce. Then another. Mueller learned the identity of the third man when he reached the top landing and stood before the bell's thick knotty beam. Captain Alonzo stood across the center well, a slight man in a trim suit whose worry filled the space. Mueller didn't see everything at once. Sweat blurred his vision, and he bent over gasping for breath, feeling dizzy and faint. Then he raised his eyes and was suddenly aware that he had interrupted the men. Clues sorted themselves in his mind and he felt the calculus of danger.

Toby Graham knelt on the stone floor. Captain Alonzo was a few feet away with a handkerchief at his lips and he pointed a snub-nosed pistol at Graham's temple. Frank Pryce made his presence known when he moved around the bell and took a position to block Mueller's escape. Pryce's white linen suit was dark with perspiration, his legs were spread comfortably, and he stared at Mueller. Mueller saw the man's tan shoes, and later he would remember his only thought was that Pryce had the largest feet he'd ever seen. Giant leather shoes, and in that moment, Mueller knew that his exhaustion made him a little delirious.

'Don't do anything stupid,' Pryce said.

Mueller took two breaths, then a third longer one, and slowly rose to full height. It was Pryce's ways of condescending to Mueller that gave him pause. It was typical of that stratagem of law enforcement that conducted itself according to the principle of threat and response. Where he needed an outcome, he bullied one. When he needed permission, he repudiated it. This obstinate behavior was offensive to Mueller. It made him forget his cooperative nature, and he found himself with his fist clenched, wanting to punch Pryce, to punish him. He indulged a sadistic thought, but said nothing.

Mueller had surprised Captain Alonzo, just as he himself had been surprised when he arrived on the scene. Not knowing everything he needed to know about what he saw, he nodded, and he kept an eye on the snub-nosed pistol. Captain Alonzo was vibrantly calm, brooding with menace, and his eyes greeted Mueller with the kindness of evil. It had been a month since he'd gotten Captain Alonzo's lecture on the inconvenience of certain truths and he had begun – almost unconsciously – to catalog the truths of Cuba. The violent sun, the poverty, the music, the torture. And now to that list he added treachery. The Cuba he had found was not the Cuba he expected to find – but then he thought: *evil does not betray you.*

Mueller saw Captain Alonzo raise the pistol and take aim. Graham's face was a mix of confusion and fear – the stunned look of the condemned man feeling the rope around his neck. Graham stared at Mueller with contempt. Mueller felt the anger, but the compounding jeopardies and his own confusion were paralyzing and left him with no words of solace.

Captain Alonzo coughed once, clearing his throat of gagging mucus, and dabbed his lips with the cotton handkerchief. He put the cloth in his pocket and turned again to Graham. 'Look away,' he said calmly. 'It's better if it's not in your face.'

'This wasn't the agreement!' Mueller yelled.

'Stay out of it,' Pryce said. 'You're in over your head. You don't have a clue what's going on.'

At the base of the tower a priest pulled the rope, and the bronze bell swung ponderously on its hinge to meet the iron clapper, producing a deep, resonant booming note that banished all other sound. Graham had started to speak, but his words were lost to the tolling bell.

It all happened in one moment. Mueller did what he had to do, what he'd trained for, without thinking and without hesitation. His face had the calm visage of an assassin. He had killed men twice. His metamorphosis in the first kill had been the caterpillar breaking out of its carapace. He'd left behind the deep thinking desk man with the squeeze of a trigger. His second kill had come more quickly and more easily. He had only one conscience to numb, one soul to subvert. The sin of the first murder was deep enough to contain a whole lifetime of killing.

Mueller's hand had gone to his Colt pistol, wedged under his belt. He brought it to eye level, gripped with his second hand, arms locked and extended, as he had practiced on Sunday afternoons at the campus gun range. He fired twice. The first bullet struck Captain Alonzo in the shoulder, causing him to drop the pistol, and the force spun him around. The second bullet entered his astonished face just below the eye. The force of that blast pushed Captain Alonzo to the tower's edge, and then he tipped backwards and fell to the street.

Mueller turned at the sound of his name. Pryce was ten feet away with his pistol raised. Pryce was livid. 'I don't bargain. Put the gun down. Men have died with the guns he brought in.'

Mueller's eyes and ears were companion witnesses to the

attack. A gun discharged loudly behind Mueller, and Pryce stiffened. Graham had taken Captain Alonzo's pistol from the floor and shot Pryce in the forearm. Mueller walked around the clanging bell and found the big FBI agent on his back. He had propped himself on his good elbow, and he coveted the pistol that had fallen just beyond reach. Somehow he knew what Mueller would do even before Mueller acted. His eyes pleaded for mercy, and he raised his palm to protect his face. Mueller hesitated. No good would come from all that had happened here. His own jeopardy was palpable. One dead Cuban. A wounded FBI agent. Mueller realized that Pryce was not the clean cop he claimed to be, but he was the sum of his corruptions. That is what the director had said. Mueller cursed his life that it was for him to right this wrong and mete out justice to this wretched creature. He closed his eyes. He knew that if he let in pity he was lost. The germ of mercy would corrupt his resolve. A silent prayer passed his lips, and he fired once. The big man shuddered violently and looked at Mueller with amazement and anger. Vile words spilled from his lips in a torrent of curses, and Mueller fired again. Somewhere in the distance was the sound of a siren, but Pryce heard nothing now, and a rush of rude blood from his mouth soiled his linen suit. Mueller dropped to his knee and placed two fingers on Pryce's carotid artery to confirm death. He had fired into Pryce's chest. Pryce would leave Cuba a good-looking corpse. Mueller owed him that little bit of dignity.

Mueller remembered Graham, but when he turned, he saw that Graham was gone. There were only the urgent footsteps of a man taking the stairs three at a time. 'Toby!' he yelled. He listened, waited, and pondered. Outside, he heard guns being fired into the air by grieving men, and he heard cries of distress. Mueller saw a small crowd gathered around Captain Alonzo's body splayed on the street in the shape of a hooked cross. Several bystanders had hands over their eyes, and looked up at the tower to see where the body had fallen from. One pointed. Confusion claimed the small crowd. No one knelt to help the stricken policeman. All gazed at the bloody, broken body with curiosity and contempt. One spat.

Mueller pulled back from the edge so he wouldn't be seen. He glanced around the bell tower, quiet now. He wasn't sure what he looked for, but he had the presence of mind to search for any evidence that might connect him to the scene. Then he looked at his watch. It was 6:02 p.m. Somehow the time seemed important. A detail, he thought, that would be important for the report he'd write. Already he was assembling a false narrative of the incident.

Moments later, he found himself in the cloisters' garden. The altar boy was gone and wouldn't be a witness. Mueller didn't want the horror of that choice. He returned his Colt to his belt, took a calming breath to clear his mind of all the death, and strolled through the garden to the exit, a casual visitor moving through the sacred place marveling at the flower beds.

He approached the parked Land Rover from behind, first looking back down the narrow alley to see if there was anyone suspicious, and when he saw no one, slipped in the back seat. He was surprised Katie and Liz were still there. Had it been only ten minutes?

Liz turned and looked at Mueller. 'Everything okay?'

He smiled, desperate that none of his gruesome work mapped to his face. 'I think so,' he said. 'We'll see. Shall we go?'

13

SWIMMING POOL

EARLY THE NEXT MORNING. Mueller woke up just after dawn and knew something had changed. It was more than his unsettled memory of the holocaust in the bell tower. It was the urgent voice of Maximo speaking outside his window. He had a heightened pitch to his instructions and then there was the sound of someone running in the courtyard. Further away, a cock trumpeted dawn and there was the laboring engine of a tractor. Mueller sat up in bed. He listened.

The door to his room was wide open, as he had wanted to attract a cooling breeze against the evening's torpor. He dressed quickly, Colt pistol stuffed under his belt, ears alert to the several voices below. When he got to the kitchen he found the breakfast table abandoned after being half set, a sudden interruption of the morning routine. The morning paper lay on the table with its headline of the latest news of the war. He glanced at the first paragraph, but shifted his attention to people scurrying in the courtyard. He looked through the kitchen, through the open library doors, and beyond to the swimming pool. The old caretaker had a lawn rake that he carefully extended in long reaching motions onto the surface of the water.

There was something floating in the middle of the pool. On second glance, Mueller saw that it was a body. Mueller made his way through the library and approached the pool cautiously. Then he saw it was Toby Graham. Graham was dressed as he had been the day before. His shoes weighed him down so that he was not so much floating as he was vertical in the water, his head below the surface, his hair arrayed like loose netting. Water around his head was stained a diluted crimson. Maximo was urgently trying to reach the body to draw it from the center to poolside, but his rake didn't have the reach, and each time he thrust it forward it fell short. He was a small man with short arms. Graham stayed in one spot in the middle.

Mueller thought they'd have to find a longer pole, or someone would have to jump in and pull the body – a thought he did not find appealing. His disbelief grew as the reality of the scene sank in. Toby Graham's death settled things, but there was nothing convenient about it, except, perhaps, the several threads that he had been unspooling would now stop. And it relieved Mueller of his unwanted obligation. Mueller's surprise was brief, as was his relief – a passing mood he would keep to himself.

There was a part of him that believed Toby Graham was not dead, merely pretending, a practical joke from which he would awake, head rising suddenly from the water to suck in a deep breath and laugh at Mueller's appalled surprise. Hadn't Graham already died once in a swimming pool? Resurrected once. Why not twice?

Out of an excess of caution Mueller looked closer at the body and saw Graham's face, gray-toned, bloated, eyes open and unfocused. Yes, he thought, death owned him now. The bullet had entered his forehead and exited explosively from the rear of his skull.

And then it started to rain. Mueller felt drops on his shoulders and rain pelted the pool's surface. An urgency to get him out of the pool before the coming downpour hit overcame the squeamishness of touch. The drama of the storm made it seem important to act, but, of course, Mueller thought, it made no difference to the corpse. But it made a difference to Maximo and the maid, who joined them, and the two gentle people pushed and prodded with additional poles brought from the verandah. It seemed disrespectful to leave Graham in the pool to be rained on.

The body was heavy and rigid. All the violence of the act of murder was gone, and whatever his desperate final thrashing moments of life had been, they remained locked in the water's memory. A cotton towel was draped over the corpse, but a second was needed to complete the shroud. Graham was laid just under the overhang beyond the drenching rain.

Liz insisted on viewing the body. Mueller was the one who woke her and he was surprised when she didn't break down in weeping shock, but then she was herself just gaining consciousness, and the news came to her as she opened her eyes from sleep. Her expression suggested she expected bad news and had already accepted the consequence. Their near-death experience in Guatemala had been a rehearsal.

Everyone remembered hearing an airplane flying low, startling the sleeping hens. Maximo said that an hour later he heard a single report in the night – now in hindsight the report of a gun – but in the cloying dreaminess of sleep it could have been the backfiring of a truck that was so common among old farm vehicles.

Mueller lifted the towel for Liz, who stood in bathrobe, arms tightly wrapping her chest. She gazed down at the gray face with kindness. 'Toby?' His name slipped from her lips.

Her lover did not reply. All the words that were to be said between them – the full text of their entire relationship – had already been said. Their world was done, finished. They had felt everything they would ever feel. Liz's grief was green and numb.

Jack had been awakened by the commotion and he emerged from his study where he'd slept on the couch, rejected by Liz. He stood at the door open to the courtyard and understood instantly the meaning of the small group gathered around the body.

He addressed his wife as she passed him heading into the house. 'Liz, you okay?'

She continued past him without any kind of acknowledgment and disappeared into the kitchen. There was the sound of quiet weeping.

PART III

1

HAVANA

WHO KILLED TOBY GRAHAM?

That was the question that Mueller addressed in his brief report to the director, which he completed in one sitting after meeting the extended deadline for the *Holiday* magazine article. Circumstances conspired against an article boosting Cuba's tourism. The lush life of acceptable sin in a tropical paradise was a hard picture to credibly portray when angry crowds were tearing down casinos' neon signs. Mueller shifted his perspective and wrote not as a tourist, but as a traveler. It was a distinction, he explained to his editor, between sitting in an air-conditioned casino with a tall drink and a shortening stock of chips, and making a rendezvous with an angry local who insults you and then pleads his story. The first is more costly, the later more exhilarating. Both are memorable. You do one in the company of others and the second alone. Alone you are an invisible observer. You can eavesdrop and see more of a place, its sadness, its people, its truth. And being the solitary traveler in Cuba, he wrote, was the best way to encounter the unexpected adventure.

Mueller still had this thought in mind when he drafted his report to the director, but he substituted the word 'outcome' for the word 'adventure.' The unexpected outcome, he wrote.

'There is no way to definitively say who killed Graham, except I can state with confidence it wasn't Pryce, and I can say with equal confidence that he didn't kill himself. I collected his things – what little he had – and nothing in his personal effects pointed to a depressed man. Quite the opposite.'

Mueller wrote: 'He had organized his life for the next phase. He believed he had a role to play. He had observed three revolutions in the short span of four years. Hungary, Algeria, Lebanon. He saw the larger truth of national movements fighting tyranny and he saw the revolutions fail. Hungary failed to the Soviet tanks. Brother fought brother in the Algerian conflict. Spontaneous hopeful riots were quashed in Beirut. He thought the Cuban revolution was the most significant revolution of them all, and he felt he had a role to play. The Cubans continued to hope and fight for a better world. The catch, of course, was that we are officially backing the wrong horse – and that bothered Graham. He had brought too much darkness into himself and I believe he wanted to find a way to hold on to his humanity. He'd never admit that – he'd laugh at it – but he thought he had a role to play keeping an open channel to the July 26th Movement. That was his game. Give them Czech guns and M1 Garands.'

Mueller had written the word 'game,' but it poorly captured Graham's serious intent, so he crossed it out and replaced it with 'desire.'

Mueller did not mention in his report two things that he found among Graham's personal possessions. There was a tattered leather King James Bible meant for traveling. It was small, with thin pages and tiny print. Mueller was surprised when he opened a cloth pouch and found it. He'd never heard Graham discuss religion, and in the absence of any obvious affection for Christianity he assumed Graham had no use for it. And Mueller realized he'd made the mistake of projecting his own skepticism onto the man. Religious? Graham? No, that was not how Mueller thought about him.

He had thumbed the pages and stopped at one underlined passage in Second Corinthians 5. 'Therefore if any man be in Christ he is a new creature: old things pass away; behold all things are become new.'

Mueller had read the passage twice and then he read it a third time. First, as a professor might, beholding the King James version in action – words from a doubly alien culture of Greek and Hebrew texts made to sound in translation as they were meant to be heard, majestic and intimate, the voice of the soul. His second reading was as an acquaintance. Mueller had dropped the charade of referring to Graham as a friend. Friendship presumed some level of familiarity, but as he had gotten closer to Graham he found only things – stubborn things – that he had not known about the man. A man at war with himself. No priest at his side. And with his third reading Mueller paused on the words 'old things pass away; behold all things are become new.' He read into the words a call to action.

The other thing Mueller did not put in his report was the handwritten note Liz had left behind in the Guatemala hotel room when she left Graham. It was scribbled in her cursive script on a small bit of hotel stationery. It was brief, said little, offered a thank you. It wished him a good life. She had signed it with her name without any endearment. Mueller had found the folded letter in the Bible. The fold was creased brittle and the edges of the paper worn from touching. Inside, there was an old photograph of a young, glamorous Liz, a large hat above her smiling face. The photograph fell out when Mueller unfolded the letter. On the back she had written, 'Thank you. Goodbye.'

'Who killed Toby Graham?' Mueller wrote. 'There was a witness interviewed by a police detective, the same one who investigated the car accident, and the embassy sent someone to observe. The ambassador flew out to add gravitas to the event and show public support among the dwindled community of expats. Everyone wanted to pretend that Americans and their property were safe and the embassy would protect them. But the actual investigation was a local matter and it was done by the detective with help from the Policía Militar. It was a perfunctory effort at best, and I believe their work was colored by their suspicions about Graham. The continuing advance of July 26th Movement forces in the weeks that followed diminished their interest. The witness was a ranch hand who had been up late drinking. The ranch hand saw a young man, slightly built, wearing a suit, enter the courtyard gate, and there was a loud crack. The young man emerged a few minutes later and ran to a waiting car.

'Graham was assassinated, of course. The assassin was that young man. I can't be certain who he is, but I suspect he is the dead girl's brother, Romolo Betancourt. I am less confident about the motive. He might have heard a rumor that Graham had been driving the Land Rover when it struck his sister, but although Graham was in fact the driver, no one outside the four of us in the car knew that. It is also possible Betancourt went there to kill Jack Malone and made a mistake. Graham had gone back to get Liz. His DC-3 arrived that night and he'd come to the house to take Liz to the airport to leave together. But upon entering the courtyard he was seen by Betancourt, who mistook him for Jack Malone. It was late, the patio was dark, and the sight of an American was enough. Betancourt fired once. I believe this is most likely what happened. The gun fired was Czech made, the model CZ52 that used 9mm shells, one of which was found in the bottom of the pool. The murder weapon was found in the driveway by a hibiscus plant, where it had been thrown. It's the type of gun Graham put in the hands of the rebels.'

Mueller ended his report with a few anodyne observations that he knew would live on in some forgotten archive, read once by the director and then never retrieved from the vault. But Mueller felt an obligation to offer a summing up – a poor version of the eulogy Graham never got – his body buried outside the walls of the Catholic cemetery in Camaguey.

'A good man,' Mueller wrote. 'I liked him, but I never really knew him. Now he is dead.'

Mueller folded his hand-written report into an envelope that would go into the embassy mail pouch. He looked over at the slim package. The death of a spy in a war zone was a lonely thing.

*

Mueller got his response from the director a week later. It came on the director's letterhead addressed personally, scribbled in the man's cramped style.

'Your note gratified me. I hadn't asked for it, but I was glad to have it. A goddamned awful mess we've made of things from what I can see. There's no evidence Castro's a communist, but I've got a senator making gloomy, slanderous predictions that Che Guevara is a convinced Marxist and it is only a matter of time before Castro consolidates power and shows his Marxist-Leninist stripes. There is abundant rhetoric and abundant lack of wit in his claims – and soon we'll know if that crab can walk backward.

'Yes, soon things will reveal themselves and we'll all know the truth. I for one suspect he is a self-serving dissembler who will find an after-the-fact argument to suggest his turn to Marxist-Leninism had been his intention all along, so he can insinuate a consistency of thinking when in fact he's made a sharp turn. The guns we had Graham deliver were a bold, noble effort. I never thought it would succeed, but Graham convinced us to give it a try. Castro played us, I suspect. He's a wily lawyer who talks his enemies into a defeated stupor. That sort of nonsense is harmless on a soapbox, but dangerous in a head of state.

'I didn't expect you to get to the bottom of the Toby Graham question. If you'd simply kept Pryce off our backs I would have considered your effort a success. I never trusted the sonofabitch. Too eager to embarrass us. But you did what I wanted you to do. You kept Pryce off balance so he was never certain what we were up to – and when he did catch on it was late in the game. I could have been more forthright with you when I asked you to fly down, but if you'd known what we were up to you would have carried a terrible burden. Better to be in the dark and confused than in the know and conflicted. Right? That's it. Now you know.

'But you also gave me a view of what got Graham up in the morning and why he did what he did. I am grateful that you gave yourself that task, and provided your conclusions. We owe loyal men little but expect a lot in return, and few ever share their innermost thoughts – or doubts – about the work they do. Your note gave me things to think about. How should we manage the faith of men who join our ranks?

'Let's have another drink when you get back. It's good to have your view. I have come to the dangerous time in my life when I look forward to reminiscing about the good old days – when we were young, naïve, green, and bull-headed about our mission. A little of that is still there – everything but the young part.

'I was surprised to hear Pryce was killed. I understand you weren't able to investigate, and frankly, given Castro's victory, I suspect we'll never know what happened. I don't think I told you, but we put in a good word for Pryce and formally commended him for his work on Graham. I was willing to be magnanimous to keep our secret. He was on to us and that's not a story we wanted out. We made sure he got posthumous credit for rolling up a threat that wasn't a threat.

'Graham knew what he was doing even if we did not at first, although he got us to come aboard. It's hard to lose a man of initiative and principle. Or, perhaps, if I am unkind, he was already lost to us and that may be the case, if everything you said about him is true. Life is ludicrously complex at times and full of cruel ironies, as you pointed out. Honor is elusive. You said he wanted to be a new man. He might have had his Agency work on his conscience, but as I've said before, we are not in the conscience business. Too much conscience makes a man a coward. We all like to think of ourselves as better than we are. It's that deception that keeps us from depression. The shrinks would have a field day with that thought.

'Graham came to believe we've made an unutterable mess of the world and that our passage through it is bitter and unheroic. I know that because he said that to me a year ago. I said that if he was a tree he could take a stand, but he was a spy and it was not his job to stand out. I'm rambling. I know I didn't tell you all this at our lunch meeting at Harvey's. I didn't want to prejudice the assignment, but you should know it now, given the outcome.

'I think he would be appalled that we would try to appropriate his outrage for a mission to cozy up to Castro. Or, he might have found humor in the preposterousness of it. For him the horror of our work was always deeply illuminating. He sought absolution and it condemned him. George, get in touch when you're back in town.'

Mueller placed the director's letter in an envelope and made sure that he found a safe hiding place for it among the folded clothes of his open suitcase. On top of the clothing he placed the *Time* magazine issue with the photograph of Castro in his mountain camp, which had come in the same pouch as the director's letter.

Nothing the director said or wrote was ever transparent or straightforward. Mueller knew that the director's calibrating mind took refuge in allusive meaning. It was the mind of a man who kept secrets. Mueller was certain the truth in the letter lay between the lines and not in the text on the page, and the letter might well be a remote act of hypnosis to shade how Mueller thought of the entire episode. A magician's trick. When the director admitted something Mueller knew the man was probably dissembling.

The director's note stirred Mueller's memories of Graham. Mueller thought he knew Toby Graham, and certainly he'd known the sort of facts that fill a biography: birthplace, college, military service, hobbies, the abandonment of his father, and his discernible achievements. But over the course of the time they'd been together he had discovered he knew little – perhaps nothing – of the inner man.

*

Mueller looked at the hotel room's French doors open to the balcony. Liz gazed across Havana. Mueller zipped his suitcase, but first took *Time* and placed it on the desk to show Liz, and then he joined her on the balcony.

The crowning dome of Havana's El Capitolio glowed luminously before them. A salt breeze stirred the evening and cloaked their moment of contemplation in serenity. Chopin's *Nocturnes* played somewhere nearby and the piano's bright notes mixed with the cacophony of riotous street celebrations. It was a few minutes before midnight. New Year's Eve festivities in Havana had started early in the evening and partying swept away the worried gloom of an anxious city bidding farewell to one calamitous year as it waited for its uncertain future.

Mueller heard the distant hum of a propeller aircraft laboring for altitude and farther away exploding fireworks that could also be gunshots. He felt Liz shudder at the sounds and he saw her look in the direction of the noise.

Across the harbor channel the limestone walls of El Morro were refulgent and pink in spotlights. Beyond the spit of land the Caribbean was a great dark oblivion. Pale breakers crumpled into mournful surf along the old sea walls that opened into the anchorage. Masts of sleek sailing yachts moored in the calm water rose and fell in the wake of a brightly lit cruise ship heading out to sea crowded with escaping Americans and wealthy Cubans. The yachts' bows had shifted seaward with the arriving tide and telltales hung limp in the air. One larger motor yacht cut a course through the moored boats, and the smoke from its coughing engine made it hard for Mueller to make out the rear ensign, but Liz, who had followed Mueller's gaze, had no doubt about its nationality. Without straining to look she said, 'It's Jack. Jack's boat. He's headed to Miami.'

Mueller looked at the chubby motor yacht that moved slowly toward the open sea.

'He asked me to go with him,' she said. 'I think that was his clumsy way of putting it behind us.' She didn't go on. Her unfinished thought remained a prisoner of her reticence. 'What is the saying? "You can't go home again." Well, I don't think we ever had a home together. We had a bankrupt enterprise.' She said this carelessly.

'We built up these memories for ourselves, but memories that weren't memories but stories about who we wanted to be.'

Mueller stood beside her, but apart, intimate and silent and close enough to hear her quiet confession. He turned and looked at her with forgiving eyes, kind eyes, thinking that he knew better what had drawn her to Graham. She was not a young woman anymore. She was mature in her suffering, and wise in her life. The dim glow from the brightly lit city burnished her forehead with sadness. Her hair was loose and fell to her shoulders, almost pale in the light.

'You worked with him, didn't you? You knew him well,' she said. Her hand clasped the photograph Mueller had taken from Graham's Bible and returned to her.

'I knew him less well than you think. His work didn't let us get close. You don't get close to anyone doing what he did,' Mueller said.

'But you admired him, didn't you? He admired you. He told me he thought you were the most honest man he knew.'

Mueller paused. 'The men he knew lied for a living.'

'But he thought of you as a friend. He must have if he gave this to you,' she said. She gazed at the frayed photograph.

He didn't give it to me. 'We were acquaintances more than friends. There was much about him I didn't know, that he didn't show me, things that he might not have known about himself. How well can you ever know anyone?' He paused. 'What are we anyway, but a bit of chemistry burdened with consciousness, who find ourselves here in this moment on the balcony looking out at a city feeling the tremor of change.'

She drew her arms around her chest. 'I'm cold,' she said. 'Hold me.'

It was warm out and she was cold. He took her obstinate grief in his arms.

'I miss him,' she said. She looked at Mueller. There was an ashen halo around her eyes. 'Do you understand that I loved him?'

Mueller wiped a tear from her eye.

'Of course.' *A lie.*

'He wanted to improve the world.'

'We all do.'

She took a deep breath. Her skin seemed to catch the luminous glow of the city and her face became solemn. 'All his kindness, his doubt, his desire, and all his promise are gone. Nothing remains except this.' She fingered the keepsake bracelet, gazing at the frayed string. 'One thing remains,' she said. 'His work.

The things he did here in Cuba live on. No one can take that away from him.'

'Of course,' Mueller mumbled. 'Noble mission.'

'A noble heart.'

Mueller wanted to tell her the truth – the evil he'd done would live on in the world and only his good was interred with his bones. He wanted to describe the world of lies that Graham inhabited, the lies to her, but in the moment, he allowed himself to believe that she knew Toby Graham best of all and he would accept her version of his life. It was the version Mueller preferred.

'You loved him too,' she said.

Mueller pondered her remark, but didn't say 'yes' or 'no,' and instead he let the thought that came to mind slip from his lips. 'Of course.'

'Hug me tighter.'

He did.

They stood there on the balcony for a few minutes. Clouds had swept in and dimmed the stars and turned the night gloomy and dark and threatening, but the two of them stood there looking out at the rioting city – distinct, apart, silent. Neither of them moved for a long time. Mueller thought he should keep thinking of not thinking of her to clear his mind and avoid a mistake if he spoke.

She suddenly turned to him. 'You're awfully quiet.' She looked at him with fierce eyes. 'Don't ask me what's next. I don't know.'

She slipped the bracelet from her wrist and let it go over the balcony. It drifted down like a feather, moving one way then the other, carried on a breeze, turning round and round and then back again, and then it was swept up by a sudden gust and taken away. She returned to the hotel room.

Mueller stayed on the balcony, elbows on the railing, feet planted, eyes fixed on the far vanishing point where dark ocean and black night were welded in a joint, and he stayed there without moving until the kiss of the moment faded.

ACKNOWLEDGMENTS

William Morgan was a U.S. citizen who fought in the Cuban Revolution, leading rebels of the Second Front who drove the Cuban army from key positions in the central mountains, helping Fidel Castro's forces defeat President Fulgencio Batista's army. Morgan was among two dozen U.S. citizens who fought in the revolution, and one of only three foreign nationals (another was the Argentine Che Guevara) to rise to the army's highest rank, comandante. Morgan's short, tumultuous life inspired the character Toby Graham, but unlike Morgan, who was executed by a Cuban firing squad after suspicions arose that he worked for the CIA, Graham's death is neither heroic nor intentional.

Morgan arrived in Cuba in December 1957 when Fidel Castro's July 26th Movement had established itself as a small but effective opponent to Batista's corrupt regime. Like many Americans, Morgan was drawn to Cuba after reading *New York Times* reporter Herbert Matthews's front-page account of meeting Castro in the Sierra Maestra mountains and his romanticized description of the bearded six-foot-tall revolutionary who was 'an educated, dedicated fanatic, a man of ideals, of courage,' who had 'strong ideas of liberty, democracy, and social justice.'

Morgan was a big, flamboyant man, who came of age in the Cold War, and like an earlier generation of young men who volunteered for the Republican cause in the Spanish Civil War, he wanted to make a difference in the world. He found his cause in Cuba's struggle. Morgan's role drew interest from the U.S. media and various U.S. government agencies, including the FBI, the State Department, and the CIA. Morgan served under Castro until he was accused of being a CIA spy. After a brief trial he was executed at dawn on 11 March 1961, in La Cabaña, the eighteenth-century stone fortress that overlooks Havana Harbor. He was thirty-two.

Several characters in the novel quote or paraphrase lines of prose. The sources are:

William Shakespeare: 'A knavish speech sleeps in a foolish ear,'

'Give me the ocular proof,'

'I have seen tempests when the scolding winds have rived the knotty oaks,'

'I wasted time and now doth time waste me,'

'Why, then, 'tis none to you, for there is nothing either good or bad, but thinking makes it so,' and 'The evil men do lives on after them. The good is oft interred with their bones'.

Ernest Hemingway: 'The world is a fine place and worth fighting for and I hate very much to leave it.'

Several books and magazine articles were indispensable sources of information about the Mafia in Cuba, rivalry between the CIA and the FBI, and the final days of Castro's uprising against Batista's regime. They are: *The Closest of Enemies*, by Wayne Smith (W.W. Norton & Company, 1987); *Havana*

Nocturne, by T. J. English (HarperCollins, 2008); *What's A Woman Doing Here?* by Dickey Chapelle (William Morrow & Company, 1962); *The Last American Rebel in Cuba,* by Terry K. Sanderlin (AuthorHouse, 2012); *The Winds of December,* by John Dorschner and Roberto Fabricio (Coward, McCann & Geoghegan, 1980); *Wedge,* by Mark Riebling (Simon and Schuster, 2002); *Havana Fever,* by Leonardo Padura (Bitter Lemon Press, 2009); 'The Yankee Comandante,' by David Grann, *The New Yorker,* 20 May 2012.

Will Roberts created a place in the world for the book by the sheer force of his intelligent suggestions. Emily Bestler provided support and encouragement, and her keen editorial touch polished and deepened the final work. The entire Atria team, particularly David Brown and Lara Jones, have been marvelous partners.

I am grateful to the Neumann Leathers Writers Group – Mauro Altamura, Rachel Friedman, Brett Duquette, Aimee Rinehart, Amy Kiger-Williams, and Dawn Ryan – for reading early drafts. Jayne Anne Phillips, Steven Schiff, Carin Clevidence, Alex Miller, Brendan Cahill, and Kelly Luce have been gracious with their support and encouragement. The book would not have found its audience without the knowing counsel of Lauren Cerand. My sons Joe and Arturo opened my eyes to aspects of the world that I had not before seen and I have benefited in my life and work from their love. And to my wife, the very special Linda Stein, partner, teacher, muse, and now collaborator. She first introduced me to William Morgan.